THE SILENT MIAOW

THE

Picture Story

by

SUZANNE SZASZ

SILENT MIAOW

A Manual for Kittens, Strays, and Homeless Cats

Translated from the Feline

and Edited by

PAUL W. GALLICO

CROWN PUBLISHERS, INC., NEW YORK

CONTENTS

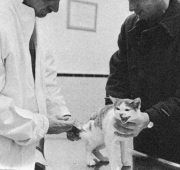

LIBRARY OF CONGRESS CATALOG CARD NUMBER: 64-17839
ISBN: 0-517-503050

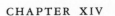

EDITOR'S FOREWORD

THE ORIGINAL MANUSCRIPT for this handbook came to me under most unusual circumstances. It was given to me by a neighbor of mine, the editor of a large publishing house that has a department specializing in educational books. One day, while he was at breakfast, the doorbell rang and he answered it himself, thinking it might be the morning papers, which were late. To his surprise there was no one at the front door, and instead of the expected dailies, a thick roll of typescript reposed on the mat.

As a publisher he was used to scripts being delivered in unorthodox ways, but he was puzzled to see the street quite empty and devoid of any retreating figure, since it had taken him only a few seconds to answer the bell. He was even more astonished when a cursory examination of the manuscript indicated that it was either the work of a lunatic, a madman or hoaxer, or a book of some kind written entirely in code of an uncommon type.

Unable to make head or tail of it, but knowing of my interest in ciphers and the fact that during the war I had had some experience in decoding, he turned the manuscript over to me in case it would amuse me sometime to attempt to solve it.

I reproduce herewith a photostat of the first page:

£YE SUK@NT MUWOQ
Q Nab8al Dir Kottebs Dra7d abd J¼n14dd ca6s
B7

When I wad z vety ypung kotteb 9 jad tje mosfortine ti lise mt motjer abd fymd mys4lf akone 9n tje worlf zt tje aye if s9x w44ks. Howeb45 9 qad no5 und8ly diturvrd v7 7jis dince 9 qas 8mtellihemt mot ikkfavpur4d 5esoyrdeful abd fill if condif3nce on myd3lf. Aslo 9 gad gad tje adban6age og seberql w44ks if 9mstruc689m fr9m mu motjer b3for3 jer 8nfort8mate emcounm645 296j q motervqr qt n9ght.

A quick glance was sufficient to establish that it followed no known pattern of cipher. The combination of figures and letters has always presented difficulties to cryptologists. Yet what we seemed to have here was obviously a title of some kind, a subtitle, the unfortunate loss of the author's name through obliteration, and then the beginning of a story. Intrigued, I tackled it, but found that it yielded to none of the usually applied techniques. I was forced to put it aside, due to press of work.

When, however, I returned to it a few months later, a most astonishing thing happened. I thought that I was able to read off the first sentence, or at least a kind of rhythm of words came into my head: "When I was a very young kotteb I had the misfortune to lose my mother and find myself alone in the world at the age of six weeks." Could it be that simple? And what was a "kotteb"? The same word appeared in the subtitle.

I went to my typewriter to transcribe the sentence as it appeared to me—a glance at the keyboard and eureka! The solution was in my hands, and translating it, at first slowly and then more rapidly with practice, I arrived at the following:

THE SILENT MIAOW
A Manual for Kittens, Strays and Homeless Cats
by
x.x.x.x.x.x.x.

"When I was a very young kitten I had the misfortune to lose my mother and find myself alone in the world at the age of six weeks. However, I was not unduly disturbed by this, since I was intelligent, not illfavored, resourceful and full of confidence in myself. Also I had had the advantage of several weeks of instruction from my mother before her unfortunate encounter with a motorcar at night."

But why this curious code based, as you will have no difficulty in ascertaining if you will look at your typewriter, on the proximity of letters on the keyboard to other letters and figures? And then the explanation dawned upon me. It was no code at all, and was never intended to be. People unfamiliar with the use of a type-font produce a pattern of error that is repetitive. The above, however, is a different sort of stumbling. It is exactly the kind of garbling that might be expected if the typewriter key were to be struck or depressed not by a finger, but by a five-toed paw, which in attempting to hit, say, the "a" would spread out to cover the "q," "w," or "s," so that any one of those others might make the imprint instead of the vowel sought.

With this clue at hand, further study soon revealed, as the title indicated, that this manuscript was written not by a human but apparently by a cat of superior intelligence, who lived where there was a typewriter available to her, in all probability one of those newfangled electric machines that are so sensitive that often a mere glance seems to activate the keys.

Delving further into the document brought to light the fact that the author reveals herself to be a "she," though even without this admission the sheer bitchery contained in many passages of this illuminating textbook could be ascribed only to the distaff side.

I, myself, am a cat lover, and in the past I have had several cats who have attempted to use my typewriters, or at any rate, played with them, engaged either in trying to break up my work in exactly the manner described in the chapter herein outlining such techniques, or merely amusing themselves, but nothing coherent ever resulted from this. I had often wished it might, and so sometimes I left a page of a novel or a short story half completed in the machine when I retired for the night, in my fantasy hoping that one of them would have finished it by morning.

However, I was never so fortunate as to have been taken over by a literary cat.

The further I progressed with my work of translation, and soon through practice I was able to read this manuscript almost as easily as if it had been properly typewritten, the more obvious it became that here was probably the most astonishing literary find since Daisy Ashford and *The Young Visiters*. For although the name of the author is lost forever through wear and tear, her character emerges from these pages as strongly as though she were sitting in front of you, looking you over and reflecting upon what she was going to make you do next. If it isn't exactly admirable, it is at least forceful and uninhibited, and if her judgment of the human race is less than heroic, we have probably only ourselves to blame.

Inquiries in the immediate neighborhood yielded no clue as to the identity of the author of this treatise. My publisher friend, to whom it was brought, had typewriters in his house but no cat, and indeed was not particularly fond of the species. Elsewhere on the block lived people with cats but no typewriters in their homes.

However, in canvassing cat owners over a wider area, I encountered a Mr. and Mrs. Ray Schorr, whose situation at least answered several of the qualifications. Some years ago they had been taken over lock, stock and barrel by a female cat they had named Cica (pronounced *tsi-tsa,* the Hungarian name for "kitten," Mrs. Schorr being of Hungarian extraction) under circumstances not dissimilar to those outlined in the narrative part of the manuscript, and they owned a typewriter—as it happened, an electric one.

Still, quite beyond being captivated by the grace and charm of their pet, they had never noticed any signs of superintelligence in her that would indicate her capability of not only putting together such a tract but acquiring the necessary vocabulary. This last does not lie beyond the realm of possibility, for every cat owner knows that his or her pet does learn some twenty to twenty-five words that it knows and recognizes.

As for the writing of the manuscript, the simplicity of patting a typewriter key makes it indeed feasible, as we have seen. A chimpanzee, for instance, can learn to imitate many of the mechanical actions of man, and in my own opinion cats are of a far higher order of intellect than monkeys. Statisticians have revealed that if a chimpanzee is set to pecking at a typewriter long enough (it may take several million years, or it might be tomorrow) he will eventually produce *Love's Labour's Lost* by William Shakespeare. Anything apes can do, cats can do better, given proper facilities.

I encountered the Shorrs' cat and found her a pleasant enough animal, no more domineering and arrogant than any other of her species, but without any visible earmarks of literary genius, either. This, however, would not eliminate their pet, since any creature clever enough to formulate and write such a set of rules, would, by the very nature of the book, be smart enough to conceal the fact. All cats are secretive, and are careful not to let you know what they are thinking.

I asked the Shorrs whether they had ever heard any sounds of typing downstairs during the night. They replied that, on awakening upon one or two occasions, they thought they had, but ascribing the noise to mice or drains, had thought nothing further about it. Actual evidence, then, pointing in the direction of their cat, Cica, remains inconclusive.

By a fortuitous circumstance, however, Mrs. Shorr proved to be a well-known photographer of children, widely celebrated through her professional name of Suzanne Szasz, whose picture stories have run in *Life* and other magazines. For her own amusement she and her husband, also a photographer, had kept a picture record of their pet from the very first day of its arrival, and offered to let us draw upon their well-stocked file of photographs of Cica as practical illustrations for these lectures.

If anything, the extraordinary manner in which the text and photographs marry might be considered the strongest clue of all, leading one to suspect that this rather innocent-looking, plain little house cat might indeed be the author of this volume.

Nevertheless, this remains in the realm of speculation. That which is not at all speculative, however, is that in the very existence of this book we have a most concrete example of the manner in which at least one of these marvelous creatures, acquiring both an editor and publisher, has advanced the eventual complete feline take-over of the human race.

PAUL W. GALLICO

CHAPTER I

Take-Over

WHEN I WAS a very young kitten I had the misfortune to lose my mother and find myself alone in the world at the age of six weeks. However, I was not unduly disturbed by this, since I was intelligent, not ill-favored, resourceful and full of confidence in myself. Also I had had the advantage of several weeks of instruction from my mother before her unfortunate encounter with a motorcar at night.

After a week or so of living in the country off a most revolting diet of grubs and insects, I determined to take over a family and become a house cat, and I set about immediately to achieve my ends.

I often discussed with friends the manner in which I attained success, and since I am not affected with vanity, I was able to point out clearly the extraordinary perception behind each move and the outstanding cleverness on my part.

So impressed were they with my story that they begged me to write it down, and furthermore, perhaps codify my experiences and ideas with regard to our relationship with human beings into a set of rules and regulations for the young about to embark upon a similar career.

This I have done. But first a brief account of the manner in which I took over my own family, who shall be nameless, since it is not my purpose to embarrass them.

The combination of the two words "take" and "over" into the phrase "take-over" is only recent in human language, and perhaps had best be explained. It is used in business. A number of people own a factory or shares in a concern, manufacturing a certain product under a certain name and in a certain location. One morning they wake up, pick up the newspaper and find out that they no longer own the company, or the product, or the name, but they now belong to someone else putting out an entirely different product in another location completely. In other words, they have been taken over.

I can think of no better phrase to apply when we move in upon human beings. Overnight everything is changed for them; their homes, as well as in time their customs and habits, are no longer their own. From then on they belong to us.

You need have no fear about embarking upon such a program. It is only opportunities, methods, and people that differ. The take-over instinct is in all of us, and has enabled us to survive unaltered and dominant through thousands of years in a constantly changing world. We have always known how to look after ourselves, nor is there any limit to what we can achieve. You have only to glance back into your own history to verify this. In Egypt less than five thousand years ago we made ourselves God. Dogs could be kicked from pillar to post, but anyone who insulted or did anything to one of us had his head cut off.

Well, then. I emerged from the woods, hungry and disgusted with nature in the raw, to see, standing in a clearing, a small, pleasant-looking white house with green-painted shutters and a barn nearby, flower and vegetable garden, small grape arbor, fish pond, etc. The house and the grounds were neat and well kept, and obviously belonged to persons of some affluence. An expensive car in the garage confirmed this. You know the saying, "Sentiment opens no canned lobster." If you want to take over a poor family, that's your business. It wasn't going to be mine.

I went to the back door of the house and reconnoitered. A man and his wife

"I cried piteously."   *Reconnoitering*

"Irresistible me."

were having breakfast inside. There didn't seem to be any evidence of children about, or servants either, which was all to the good. Children are all right eventually, and can be handled, but it is better, if possible, to take over your family before they arrive. And servants can give you a lot of trouble.

This pair looked exactly like the family I wanted, so I jumped onto the screen door, clung there, and cried piteously.

They looked up at me from their breakfast. I knew exactly how I appeared to them from the other side of the screen door. Irresistible! I pretended to lose my grip on the mesh and fell off, and then climbed back up again, crying all the time.

The woman said, "Oh look! The poor little thing, it wants to come in. Maybe it's hungry. I'll give it some milk."

Just as I expected! I had her. All I needed was to get one paw inside the door and—

However, it wasn't going to be all that simple. The man!

He began to shout, roar, scrape his chair, and thump the table with his fists, bellowing that he hated cats and he wouldn't have one in the house. Then he went into all those boring clichés about how we were a nuisance, got into everything, clawed the furniture, and smelled up the joint. He kept yelling, "Nix! Nothing doing! If you've got to feed it, give it some milk in the barn and then get rid of it. But it doesn't come in here."

"Oho!" I said to myself. "You'll want some dealing with, my friend, and I'm the one who knows how to do it." You may not believe this, but I was almost pleased with this opposition. It was a challenge. If there's anything that's fun to work over, it's a man who thinks he is a real cat hater. In the meantime, while these thoughts were going through my head, I kept falling off and climbing back onto the screen door, still crying heartbreakingly.

The woman opened it and picked me off, saying to him, "Oh, don't make such a fuss, darling. I'll just give her some milk. We'll put her out afterwards."

The point, you will have gathered from this, is that the more men rage, fuss, shout, and yell, the less attention one pays to them. For although he was still clamoring and protesting, where was I? Inside the door, lapping up milk out of a saucer.

Once inside I knew exactly what to do, for my mother, who herself had a difficult person to deal with, had told me a great deal about men and how to handle them. I simply ignored him and played up to the woman, who was making all kinds of soft, cooing noises about me, calling me names like "dear," "darling," "sweet,"

"See? Inside *the screen door."*

The first hand-out

"pet," and "little angel." And, of course, the more she fussed over me the angrier he got until finally he shouted, "Okay now, that's enough! Come on, get it out of here."

The woman said to the man, "Of course, darling, anything you say," and lifting me up, put me out of doors, saying, "There now, run along, Kitty." But of course, I knew she didn't mean it, so I immediately jumped onto the screen once more and cried to come in again, until the man began to shout, "There you are! You see what you've done? Go take her over into the woods."

She did this, but as soon as she turned around, I followed her back to the house. We did this three times, while the man came out of the house with his hat on, got into his automobile, and watched us. The fourth time I just sat down at the edge of the woods and looked miserable. The man kissed his wife good-by, but the last thing he did before he drove away was to turn around to see me sitting there, all alone, by myself. I was satisfied because I was sure that I had spoiled his day, and all he would be able to think of would be me.

Of course, as soon as the car had disappeared around the bend in the road, the

"I just sat down and looked miserable."

wife came out of the house, picked me up and carried me back inside, as I knew she would. I had her where I wanted her. We had a lovely day together.

Just before evening she took me in her arms, kissed me, and said, "Now, Kitty, I'm afraid you must go. He'll be coming back." She put me out, and soon the headlights of the car came around the corner and the man came home.

I stayed until it was quite dark and then, putting myself in the right mood of feeling sorry for myself, because I was lonely and hungry again, I sat outside the screen door and just cried and cried and cried.

The light was on in the dining room. Through the window I saw them eating their supper. I went and sat under the window and cried louder.

Suddenly the man slammed down his knife and fork and shouted, "I can't stand that noise!"

The woman asked, "What noise?"

The man bellowed, "That damned cat! I told you this morning this would happen!"

Damned cat! Yes, that's how he referred to me. Well, before I was through with him I was going to have him groveling.

I put everything I had into my miaows. They would have melted a heart of stone. The woman said, "Oh, the poor little thing, she must be hungry again."

The man shouted, "For Heaven's sake then, why don't you get it in and feed it?"

The woman began, "Because you said . . ."

The man replied, "Never mind what I said! You can put it out afterwards. I can't hear myself eat with that damned yelling going on."

So the woman came out and fetched me and I had another good meal, and after dinner, instead of putting me out, the woman took me onto her lap, where she played with me and cuddled me, and I at once began to purr and make up to her. The man was reading his newspaper, but every so often he would put it down and throw us black looks.

After a while the woman put me onto her chair and went out of the room and didn't come back. I pretended that I was asleep, but instead I was watching the man, who kept looking over at me. I knew what was on his mind, all right. He was jealous. He would have liked to have taken me on *his* lap, but he couldn't admit it.

After a while the woman called down from upstairs, "Oh, darling, I'm almost ready for bed. Will you put the cat out?"

The man gave a great snort, threw his paper away, and shouted, "Me! Why can't you put it out? You got it in!"

"Darling, I've told you, I'm undressed already. Take it over to the edge of the woods."

The man bawled, "Oh, damn! All right!" and picked me up, got a flashlight, and carried me out. He was most awkward holding me, and when I got my head under his chin he mumbled, "Cut it out, Kitty," and I knew I could have had him right then and there, if I had just rubbed up against his beard a little and purred. But I wasn't in any hurry. I knew now that I could take him whenever I wanted. I made up my mind to soften him up so that when the time came he would become my absolute slave. The more rotten I could make him feel, the better. So, when he went to put me down in the woods, I just fastened my claws into his shirt and screamed.

"The man was going to take some working over."

He unfastened me and put me down. I kept on yelling as he went off, and of course, as I knew he would, he turned around and switched on his flashlight to see whether I was following him, which of course I was. He picked me up, snarling, "Goddam it, Kitty, stay there!" I anchored myself to his shirt again. We kept going through this routine. Eventually I got my head under his chin again and he mumbled, "Oh, well . . ." and I started to purr. He said, "Don't kid yourself, Kitty," and marched off with me, but this time he took me to the barn, where he rummaged about until he found an old cardboard box, into which he dumped me. He said, "There! You can stay there, and for Heaven's sake keep quiet!" Then he walked off again but couldn't resist turning around and putting the light on to see if I was going to follow him again. This time I didn't. I just sat there looking at him, with my head showing above the box, and he stood looking at me. And so I gave him the Silent Miaow.

Later in this book you will find a section on the Silent Miaow in the chapter on speech, how it is done and when it is most effective, and you will see how clever of me it was to apply it at this time, particularly since I had been doing such a lot of screaming and crying.

The effect was just what I expected. The man came all unstuck. He stood there looking absolutely helpless, saying, "For Heaven's sake, Kitty, what do you want now?"

I gave him the Silent Miaow again.

He came back into the barn looking baffled, picked me up out of the box, and said, "What the hell are you after, Kitty?" I got my head into his neck and purred like a mad thing. He said, "No, you don't. You don't come back into the house." And then, "I suppose the box isn't good enough for you. Okay, let's see what we can do." He put me down and hunted about until he found an old bit of blanket, which he shook out and made into a little nest for me. "There you are," he said, "how's that, Kitty?"

I decided that this was the time to begin training him, so I climbed back into the box. He took me out and put me onto the blanket. I got back into the box again. He lost his temper and shouted, "Oh, damn! Stay in the box, then!" and started to march out. But I knew he was going to have to look back at me again, and when he did I was ready. I crossed him up this time with a loud miaow.

He said, "For Heaven's sake, Kitty, I can't stay here all night! What DO you want?"

I let him have it again. He came back, took me out, picked up the blanket, put it into the box and lifted me back. *That* was what I wanted, and I let him know it by beginning to circle around in it immediately, making my bed and curling up there purring. He looked down at me for a moment and said, "Okay, Kitty, I get it," and went back to the house.

His wife must have been waiting at the door for him, for I heard her say, "Darling, what on earth have you been doing? You've been ages," and his reply, "I thought maybe it might be going to rain. I put the cat in the barn. She can stay there."

Ha! Ha! Ha! Me stay there! That was a good one! I laughed myself to sleep.

Of course, after that it didn't take long at all, and the very next night I thought it was time to take him.

"I decided this was the time to begin training him."

"So I climbed back into the box."

"That *was what I wanted.*"

It was a hot, sultry summer evening. I was sitting on the woman's lap interfering with her sewing (you will see my chapter on this later) and the man was reading his newspaper as usual. I got off her lap, had a good, long stretch, and went over and sat looking up at him. At first he pretended he didn't notice, but finally he put away his paper and said, "What is it you want, Kitty?"

I gave him the full treatment—the big "hello," with the rub up around the ankles. As I expected, the man came all apart. He said, "Why, you little cutie, do you want to get up onto *my* lap?" With that he picked me up and put me there and began to stroke and chuck me under the chin. I turned on the purr and the charm and gave him the works, rolling in his lap, cuddling up and giving his hand a couple of licks, spreading on the butter so thick you could slice it.

Naturally he went all to pieces and began to murmur idiot things like, "Well, what do you think you're up to, Kitty?" repeating it over and over, while throwing glances of triumph across to his wife, who just sat sewing and didn't say anything.

Just then there was a flash of lightning and a crashing of thunder and it began to pour. They went around closing all the windows in the house, the man carrying me with him, saying, "Nothing to be frightened of, Kitty old girl. Just a little old thunderstorm, that's all."

Some time later the thunder and lightning went away, but it kept on raining and the woman said, "I guess we can go to bed now. Will you put the cat out?"

The man looked at her as though she were out of her mind and shouted, "What? Put her out on a night like this? Are you crazy?"

"Why? She'll be all right in the barn, won't she? I thought you said you didn't want a cat in the house . . ."

The man was furious. "Well, I don't want a cat in the house," he roared. "But that doesn't mean putting her out in a cloudburst. Look, she's trembling like a leaf! Haven't you got any heart?"

Trembling was right. I was trying to keep from laughing out loud.

His wife shrugged and said, "All right, have it your own way. But I was only saying what you said when . . ."

"I certainly will have it my own way! We can put a cushion on the floor in the kitchen for her. "

They went upstairs to their room and I heard them moving about. After a while their light went out and the woman said, "You haven't shut the bedroom door."

The man replied, "Well, if the storm came back or anything, or Kitty was frightened, we wouldn't be able to hear her, would we?"

"He went all to pieces . . ."   *". . . and began murmuring idiot things."*

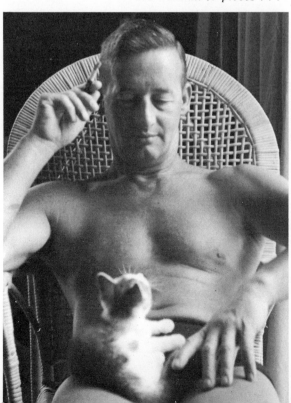

So, of course, during the night I went upstairs and got onto the bed and slept on top of the blanket underneath which his feet were, where it was nice and warm.

In the morning I woke him up by walking on his face and putting my foot in his mouth. He sat up, took hold of me, and said, "Why, you little cutie! Who asked you up here? Come on, let's have a look at you." And he began to play with me. I put my head under his chin again and purred.

His wife said, "Darling, do you think we ought to have her on the bed . . ."

He threw her a dirty look. "Why? What's wrong with that?" he said. "Look, she's nuts about me. Cats are supposed to be clean, aren't they?"

"Yes, but—"

"But what? She's on my side of the bed. I don't know what you're kicking about."

We all had breakfast in the breakfast nook downstairs in the kitchen, and I sat on his shoulder, or lay across the top of the seat behind his neck.

The man looked absolutely smug and said, "Look at the little bastard, what's got into it?"

". . . so of course I got onto the bed."

"In the morning I woke him up."

His wife said, "Not bastard, bitch. It's a she. I think she's in love with you."

This statement had the most curious effect upon the man, causing him to laugh more loudly than was necessary, fumble for cigarettes, and not know what to do with his hands. He was actually blushing. He said, "Nonsense! I just knew how to handle her last night during the storm. She's grateful."

I cruised back and forth along the top of the seat, rubbing against his neck and purring. When he went off to work that morning he kissed his wife good-by, said "So long, Kitty" to me, and then added to her as he went out, "Look after my cat."

That night, after dinner, I got onto his shoulder when he read the newspaper and stayed there. Suddenly he put the paper down, yawned, stretched, and remarked, "Bedtime, I guess. Come on, Kitty."

Nothing was said about the barn. Nothing was said about the kitchen either. All of us went upstairs to bed.

That's the way I entered my house.

Now I will begin my book on Taking Over.

"I'm still here."

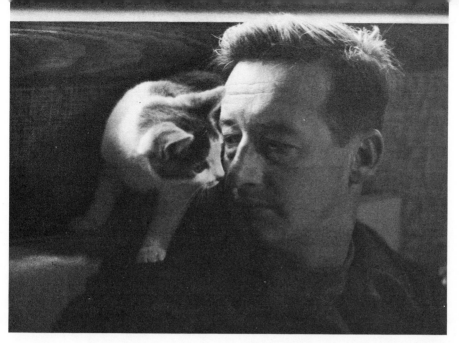

"Shoulder cruising! It works every time."

"He's in love with me."

CHAPTER II
People

Men

IN DEALING with the man of the house, it is fortunate that by and large the species suffers from a basic insecurity and is plagued, particularly in family matters, with an ambivalence that can be most usefully exploited.

Man is God the Thunderer, the Keeper of the Law, the Big Policeman, the Prosecuting Attorney, the Stern Judge, and the Executioner. But man is also God the Benign Father who cherisheth, forgiveth, loveth, and handeth out, and the point is he never knows quite or entirely which or when, and as you will have seen from the chapter on my own experiences, can be manoeuvered in the twinkling of an eye by a clever woman, or even sooner by a clever cat, to reverse himself.

You may have reached the conclusion that because of all his shouting, banging, and yelling, my man did not like his wife, but this would be erroneous. That is simply how men are. They roar, bellow, order people about, and issue edicts, and their women let them because they know that after they have finished they usually feel rotten and will do what the woman wanted in the first place. The trick is always to let them *think* they are having their own way.

Men, because they are God, are terribly jealous. That was what was the matter with my man, as you may have guessed. He actually loved the woman—human love, I refer to, the kind I will discuss in a later chapter, but he didn't want anybody or anything else to love her, or her to pay attention to anyone but him. Why, very often they are even jealous of their own children. If you understand this you will never make the mistake in a household of becoming merely *the* cat. Whenever he is around you will be *his* cat.

"Your prerogative."

"Nothing to it! The man is absolutely besotted."

You will also find that in any family, no matter how much the man and wife love one another, there is always a rivalry between them, so that you can play one off against the other. If the woman scolds you for something you have done, the man will immediately take your part and say, "Poor Kitty! She couldn't help it." If the man loses his temper or gets annoyed with you, the wife will be on your side.

One of the most important things you have working for you to subdue and keep in his place the man, your man, any kind of man, is the fact that we are wholly independent and hard to get. You must never forget this.

For, as I have pointed out, man is so basically insecure that he must be constantly loved, admired, flattered, and fawned upon. That's how dogs get away with it. That's why when he finds one woman who will do all this for him, he completely loses his head and gives her all his money, a house to live in, jewels, presents and things, and will work from morning until night.

Well, we don't and they know it.

"You will learn to put up with a certain amount of idiocy."

But that is why when we do give him a little affection or soft-soap him for something we want, it is a hundred times more effective. Let him hold you in his arms while lying on your back and see the absolutely besotted expression that will come over his countenance. Or assume the same position on his lap, or curl up and go to sleep on him and he won't move for hours on end for fear of disturbing you, or until he gets a muscle cramp. Take the trouble to be waiting for him at the door when he comes home and he will pick you up and give you the big "hello" before even bestowing a kiss upon his wife. Men are so grateful to be able to think they have made a cat care for them that there is simply nothing they won't do for you. For instance, I induced mine to make four sleeping boxes for me before I finally accepted the last one and he was so happy when I curled up on it that he almost cried.

Ways and means of buttering up the man are discussed in various other places of this volume, and you will, of course, find your own. Follow him when he goes for a walk in the garden or the woods. It is most effective. He will take it that you can't bear to be away from him for a moment. Sitting on the edge of the bathtub or the cover of the toilet seat and watching him while he shaves in the morning is another excellent gambit. And, of course, when you really want to tie him in knots, you will come when he calls you in front of other people.

"For instance, I induced my man to make four sleeping boxes before I finally accepted the last one. And then I slept on top of it instead of inside."

But, you will be saying to yourself, this is giving up independence! Not a bit of it. You are merely pretending that he is the God he thinks he is and it won't take a millimeter off your whiskers.

"Anthropomorphism" is a word you will encounter a great deal in this book, and you had best know something of its meaning. It means that people ascribe human qualities to things or to animals because they are so conceited they think the world revolves around them, and that the greatest thing on earth is to be a human being. Therefore half the time they don't think of us as cats at all but as something else, a phenomenon you will also learn to use. If you will study how to soften up your man properly from time to time, he will see you no longer as a cat, but as some kind of fur-bearing, female member of his own species who has lost her head over him, and after that you have got him where you want him.

Nicely softened up

Women

Do not, I repeat, DO NOT apply the same methods and ploys to softening up the woman of the house as you do to buttering up the man. They won't work for the simple reason that she has probably used some of them herself on the same male.

Women are a great deal like us, a comparison distinctly not in our favor, but one to be considered at all times in any dealings that you may have with them. Huntresses like ourselves, they are feral, even cruel, playing with their victims as we are accused of doing; often letting them apparently escape, and just as the unfortunate quarry is breathing a sigh of relief, and his palpitations have ceased, turning upon him and applying the crusher.

"Reflect. Don't underestimate women."

"I think of a woman as something like myself."

Do not underestimate them, for they are extraordinarily clever—far more clever, certainly, than the males they have captured and taken over. They will have known, and made use of for this purpose, as many ploys and gambits as you yourselves will have learned in order to take them over. And sooner or later you must be prepared for the fact that the moment will come when you and Madam are going to have to have it out, a moment of truth when she will know not only exactly what you have done to enmesh her husband, but also how you have done it.

Don't let this alarm you, for she will admire you and respect you for it, although it may slightly diminish her respect for her husband; but this is not your concern since the passage of time, anyway, will have a tendency to reduce this. It simply means that from then on she *knows*, and if you are wise you will not take the same liberties with her that you can permit yourself with him. However, if you will contrive to acquaint her with the fact that you know that she knows and are prepared not to get up to too many shenanigans with her, you will find yourself living in a

[39]

A comfortable and amicable state of truce

very comfortable and amicable state of truce with an unexpected ally, who can always be relied upon to side with you against him.

Think of the woman as someone something like yourself, and then you will not make the mistake of underestimating her. She is far tougher than the man, knows what she wants, and how to get it. She has a soft side that can be used when you are training her to run the house your way. Learn to know when she is bad tempered or upset about something and keep out of her way at those times.

I shall have covered most of the problems which may arise with women in the various other chapters dealing with situations you are likely to encounter in different kinds of households. Hence I will only, here, touch upon the sad case of the cat who has become so devoid of all sense of independence, as well as bereft of personal dignity, that she remains in the household of a person who is lonely and childless and consents to act as a substitute.

"You will, of course, never consent to being locked up in the house. You are entitled to be outdoors in all kinds of weather."

Grape arbors are for lurking . . .

. . . and trees for observation.

As we know, it takes all kinds to make a world, and there actually are cats so lazy, so willing to be pampered and spoiled that they not only condone, but even enjoy, this disgusting kind of life. They will consent to being locked inside the house, being made to sleep on silk cushions where every other, normal cat will prefer a piece of newspaper or sacking, and to being addressed inanely and idiotically in baby talk, or being cooed at or held up close to faces. No cat can possibly maintain its self respect under these conditions. And if ever you find yourselves so unfortunate as to come in contact with one (and they will try to justify themselves), don't believe them for a moment when they tell you that they would like nothing better than to get back onto the tiles, if they could, but they are kept indoors all the time and never let out. If you received proper educations from your mothers you will know that for a smart cat there is no such thing as being kept a prisoner in a house. Sooner or later the opportunity will present itself for escape. I always say every cat has the kind of home it deserves.

Children

By and large children are a nuisance, although I should say they come under the heading of a mixed blessing, and where children are concerned you will have to decide for yourselves whether the price is worth while. A great deal, of course, will depend upon the type of family you select, the age and sex of the offspring and the amount of discipline in the home. Small boys are worse than little girls. Where there is a child in the house you will be expected to put up with all kinds of inconveniences and indignities, which include having your tail pulled, being carried about suspended by your stomach, and being mauled unmercifully. On the other hand you might find yourself growing quite fond of one or more of them, if decently brought up. It is only when they become adults that they acquire those ridiculous characteristics that make all of them so inferior to us cats.

But the main point I shall bring out is that if the child or children love *you,* this is your insurance to be properly looked after as long as you like, and the

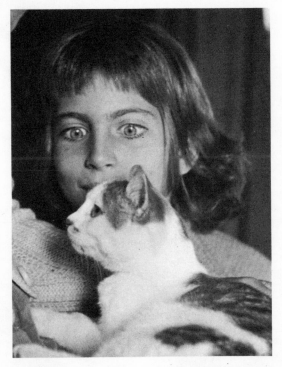

"The children rule the house."

"When you are being smothered—relax."

stronger the ties you can forge with the child the better. For you will find to your surprise that in our country, for instance, and I am speaking of the United States, it is not really the grownups who rule the household, but the children. You could not imagine this in the cat world, where, if you make one false move, your mothers knock you for a goal, and quite right, too. But people hereabouts are apparently terrified of their children and spoil them inordinately, turning them into disgusting brats, yet if you can stomach them and become known as "little Johnny's" or "darling Mary's" cat, you are safe from interference of any kind, beyond that which you will have to learn to put up with from Johnny or Mary.

A word of caution: never, under any circumstances, retaliate with tooth or claw for anything a child might do to you. For if you are so much as suspected of having scratched their Precious, even in play, you will find yourselves back in the alley before you can say *felix domesticus*. Remember at all times, when you are being squeezed, smothered, pulled, hauled, stretched, and tugged at, that it is done because *they* think you are one of them. Anthropomorphism again. Of course, if you have the bad luck to select a child that is deliberately cruel and remain around one minute after the fact has been established, you don't deserve to be a member of our species.

"Remember, small boys are worse than little girls."

The Bachelor

I have not much to say to you on the subject of bachelors, and if you decide to adopt one, I advise you first to make a thorough study of his habits and personality and then make your decision.

To begin with, there are not all that many about, and the fact is that if a man has reached the age of fifty without being able to attract some woman or another into a successful partnership with him, there is something the matter with him and he might very well not be the right material for living with a cat. On the other hand, in a bachelor of experience, who has been married and divorced, you might well find a prize. A man who has managed to get rid of a tiresome woman often finds

"One can arrange for quite a comfortable household."

"Not even a leash with a bow on it."

a cat most pleasant and rewarding thereafter, and one can arrange for quite a comfortable household, particularly if he is well off and has a housekeeper.

At the same time I must point out certain drawbacks of which you ought to be made aware. Men on their own are quite likely to drink, one of the nasty human failings with which I hope none of you will ever have to come into contact. When they drink they become completely irresponsible and unaware of what they are doing. They are useless at home and embarrassing in public.

Bachelors are also likely to become eccentric or whimsical, neither quality of which makes for the kind of life and household you should be wanting. Most bachelors, on the whole, prefer dogs, since, lacking the necessary adulation usually supplied in normal life by one woman, they find it in the dog, which, as you know, is utterly incapable of concealing the fact that it worships these absurd people. What you must be careful of in choosing a bachelor household is that he doesn't try to make a dog of you, even to the point of fitting you out with a collar and leading you about on a leash, which I should say is about the most humiliating thing that can happen to a self-respecting cat. I once knew a bachelor, a film actor, who took his cat simply everywhere—in his car, on the set, out to dinner, with him to late parties, traveling on trains and airplanes, in fact just as though he were married to her. To be truthful, I must tell you that this cat actually *liked* it. It was unnatural—I should not have been able to have stood it for a minute—but, of course, there are exceptions and it merely proves the rule that it is entirely up to you, what you choose. If she *hadn't* liked it, she could have gone away.

Shall we say that if you select a bachelor to adopt, you can expect to have to put up with a number of minor inconveniences, but life will never be dull.

"Life will never be dull."

CHAPTER III

Property Rights

The Bed

WHETHER OR NOT you wish to take over the bed is entirely up to you, and here again you will find yourself involved in that astonishing ambivalence that seems to be a part of people and that never ceases to surprise me, even while I welcome it. They won't want you on the bed, and at the same time, they *will* want you on the bed. If this is a paradox it is because that is what people seem to be like.

"I really ought to be in the bed."   *"My own daytime resting place."*

The bed is a delightful place for a sleep, particularly when there is a clean counterpane on it. You can't avoid leaving cat hairs, and often when you stretch in your sleep, or just upon waking, your claws will get caught and pull threads loose. That is when they won't want you on the bed and when laws will be promulgated forbidding it. Yet, often when they are in it they will want you on the foot of it, or even curled up close to them. Even though two people have one another they still seem to be lonely sometimes and want you for company, or when one or the other is by himself or herself. For human loneliness is one of the most powerful characteristics for winning you the kind of home and service you want. It is our particular good fortune that we are able to allay this just by being about, snoozing on the hearth before the fire, sitting up and washing, or playing quietly in some corner.

But to return to the bed, the point is they can't have it both ways. It either is or it isn't your territory, and since they can't make up their minds, it is up to you to make up yours. If you prefer the bed to your own box or chair for sleeping, establish this immediately. The chances are they will be flattered and think that it is because you can't bear to be away from them, and they will use it as a brag: "Our cat always sleeps at the foot of our bed," to which, if you like, you can get them to add, "And comes and wakes us in the morning," by simply getting up when you have had enough sleep and walking across their faces, which they seem to enjoy.

The technique for taking over the bed is simple and is all a matter, again, of timing and habit. It means seeing to it that you are in the bedroom mornings and evenings when they are *in* the bed and invite you up. Thus once you have formed their habit of seeing you there, you will have no further trouble. Another gambit is to go upstairs after breakfast and get onto the bed before it is made. You will be put off during the making of it, but as soon as this is done you get right back onto it again, and in nine cases out of ten you will be allowed to stay.

A word of warning on beds. If there is a baby in the house, don't *ever* get into its crib or indicate that you would like to sleep there. There is a legend afoot amongst people that a very young baby was once smothered to death by one of us sleeping across its face. This is, of course, utter nonsense, since the one place we never sleep is close to anyone's face. But you will find that, by and large, people actually live by the legends they invent, and it is something you must put up with and respect.

The Chair

You will wish from the beginning, after you have once established your occupancy in the household you have chosen, to select and pre-empt a certain chair for your very own, not to be used thereafter by any other member of the family and to be reserved for your use whether you need or want it then or not.

The appropriation and holding of a chair takes time, vigilance, and patience, particularly if it happens at one time to have belonged to the so-called master of the house, or stands in such a position as to be used for practical purposes, say at a desk or table, or is meant for the convenience of visitors.

To begin with, in taking the chair over for your own exclusive use, you must be prepared at first to spend a great deal of time in it, curled up sleeping, or pretending to sleep even if you are not, in order that the family accustom themselves to seeing you there. People, as you will learn, are creatures of habit and extraordinarily lazy. They can be brainwashed into believing anything and eyewashed into accepting certain situations as *fait accompli*. By eyewashing I mean *seeing* you there on the chair every day, they will soon be convinced that it is "your" chair and not "their" chair.

However, this is still a preliminary stage of the campaign, and will result in no more than their refraining from making you leave it once you are there. It won't keep *them* from using it in your absence, or if you happen not to be in it.

The next stage consists of training them to keep out of it, which calls for a week or so of great watchfulness. You will remain in the vicinity of the chair, and when anyone appears to be heading for it, you will jump up and get there first. Having arrived there, you can do one of two things to hold the position: begin washing actively, above all being careful never to catch the eye of the person who has been trying for your place, or curling up and settling yourself in a sleeping position.

If the latter, you will find it most convenient to your purpose to assume either a graceful or a "cute" pose, such as placing one paw over your nose, or lying on your back with your feet hanging limply, or any one of a number of others discussed in my chapter, "Attitudes." The object here, and it will succeed in nine cases out of ten, is to distract the person's attention from his original idea, which was to sit down in the chair. If the pose is quaint enough, other members of the family will be brought to come and look, and they may even go and fetch a camera. If they still want to sit down, they will select another chair, and possession of yours will have been impressed even more deeply into their malleable brains.

We must never forget, nor neglect to exploit, a curious advantage we enjoy over the human species by being an animal and theoretically unable to communicate with people. If you can make your wishes known it will be considered a master stroke by them, something highly amusing and for some unknown reason redounding entirely to their credit.

"And this is my *chair."*

There is a kind of vast, undefinable subtlety connected with this that is not easy to explain. But let us say the man of the house has taken your chair and you have managed to let him know that you want it, with the result that other members of the family call his attention to the fact. Interested or amused, he relinquishes it to see whether it is true, and finds out that it is and thereafter proceeds to dine out upon it, or uses it as a topper when cat stories are being exchanged. By a curious inversion the fact that you have diddled him out of his seat will enlarge his own view of himself, since the fact that *his* cat is cleverer than his neighbor's, or any other, cat can have resulted only from association with him. All right. You let him think that. *But in the meantime you will have got the chair.* If any other member of his family were to ask for it or try to sit in it, he would be told to go jump in the lake, or he would be ousted from it without ceremony. But every time you put him out of it, it is accepted as a continuing confirmation of the fact that you are a very clever cat. Which, indeed, you are.

There remains the problem of the quondam visitor who does not know, or has not yet found out. Some families are embarrassed to point out the error immediately if your place has been usurped, but if you will give them a little assistance, they soon learn to cooperate.

If you come into the room and the guest is already sitting in your place, there are various ways of making yourself disagreeable. You can sit silently and stare; you can reach up and dig your claws into his knees, or you can jump up either into his lap or onto any small space that might be left beside him and the seat, and ostentatiously try to make yourself comfortable in it. Since most people who come to call will be wearing good clothes they won't want cat hairs spread over them, and since more people don't like cats than do, the percentage chances are that you will hit upon an ailurophobe. Thus, for one reason or another you will be picked off their laps and put back onto the floor. Jump right back up again, which will give whichever member of your family is present the cue to say, "Oh dear, I'm afraid you have got Kitty's chair." This will cause the visitor to leap up as though his pants, or her dress, were on fire and take another one, mumbling that they are sorry and didn't know. Your man or woman may then further remark, deprecatingly, "Kitty's rather taken over since we've had her. We only live here," and then you will know that you have achieved the highest possible results. They have knuckled under one hundred per cent and you have made them like it.

I hesitate to pass along this final instruction, since it is definitely not nice and is to be used only as a last resort. But there are some visitors who are too self-important or thick-headed, as well as hosts who are either too shy or too hospitable to discommode a guest, and hence won't ask them to move. You cannot afford to overlook this, or in any way to diminish or cast doubt upon the established fact that this is your chair from now until eternity, for you might not only undermine that position but many others. And so I do reveal that which has rarely been known to fail. You settle down quite quietly at their feet, paws tucked under, and make a smell. Before long the visitor will get up out of the chair and go over to the window, or cross to the other side of the room and take a seat on the sofa. At this point you get up on your property, wash a few licks as though nothing had happened, curl up, and relax. If your people smell it they will never let on, for that would be almost as though they had done it.

"You heard me say this chair belongs to me, didn't you?"

Other Places and Properties

Once you have understood and mastered the ploy of what can be accomplished by being different from other cats, even to the point of eccentricity, as long as it will make a good story or a unique photograph, you can extend your domain over any place or any article in the house you might care to make your own. And this, I might suggest, also works in reverse if there is something that displeases you or for which you won't stand.

For instance, they might make you a box bed to be your own. If it is well done, comfortable, and to your liking, accept it, of course, for there is no use in cutting off your tail to spite your bottom, and you will find, likewise, that your people are thrilled over such an acceptance and the fact that they have managed to please or satisfy you.

"I have accepted this bed . . ."

". . . but it doesn't mean I can't sleep anywhere else I like."

But if you DON'T like it, have nothing to do with it. Never go near it. When put into it, get out immediately and make clear your objection by dossing down in the laundry hamper or pre-empting a bureau drawer where the handkerchiefs or Madam's underwear are kept. This last is often very effective, it makes an interesting story and yields excellent snapshots to be handed about.

Never forget that they will put up little or no resistance when you appropriate some article such as a pair of slippers to play with or chew on, or a sweater to lie upon. It may be a favorite garment belonging to him or to her, but ridiculous as it may seem, they will actually be flattered that you have appropriated it and somehow work it around to where they will take it as proof of your affection for them.

"These are now mine, too."

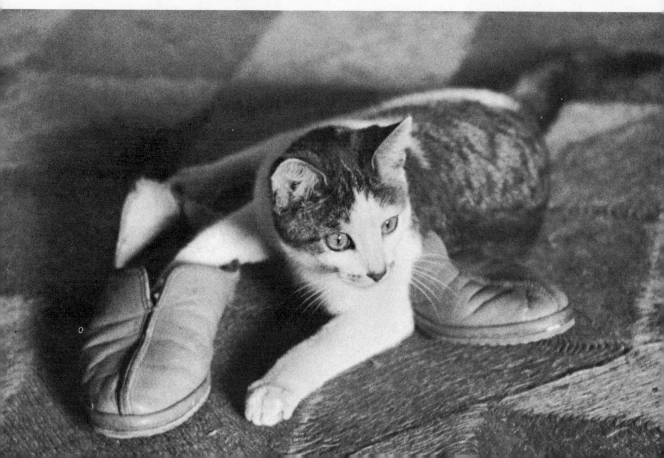

CHAPTER IV

Going to the Vet

I DON'T SUPPOSE this subject really belongs in a book of instruction on how to take over a household, but it is, after all, a part of living with people, and since the success or failure of your take-over will be judged by your relationship with them. your first and possibly subsequent trips to the veterinary is bound to come up, and a little good advice never did anybody any harm.

People spend more time being sick than you would think possible amongst a species that likes to pride itself upon being more intelligent than we are. They are always getting colds or headaches or stomach-aches, if not more mysterious, lingering, and

". . . people go breaking their legs."

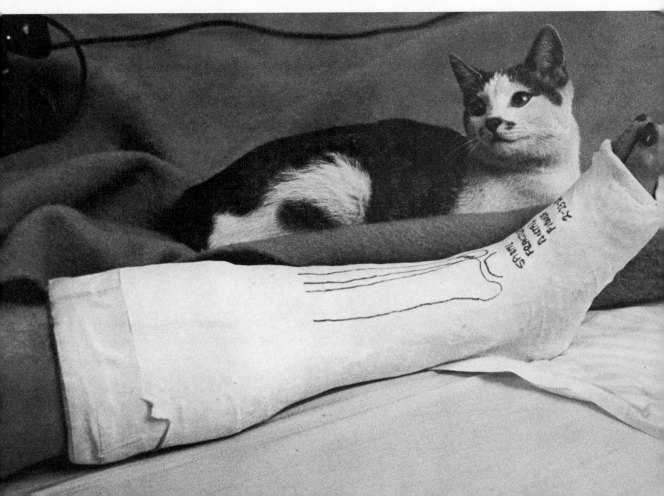

"Don't go and hide."

unpleasant diseases, or breaking their legs or arms, or getting themselves cut or bruised, and they are usually rushing off to doctors of one type or another. In fact so many things are constantly happening to them that they have special kinds of doctors for different kinds of diseases in the various places and parts of their bodies. They also spend a great deal of time imagining they are sick when they are not.

Now we are rarely ill, and if we are we go off somewhere and eat grass until we feel better, or if we get slashed up in a fight we lick the place until it heals, and that is that.

But since so many humans think of us as people instead of animals, they make up a lot of sicknesses and diseases—which we never had before, until we had to cope with steam-heated houses in winter and air-conditioned ones in summer and the filthy state in which they keep their streets—and so they are always hustling us off to the veterinary as soon as we sneeze or have a hot nose, or lie about for a day instead of tearing around the house like a lunatic.

Well, you will think from this that I am about to tell you to refuse to go to the vet, to run and hide when your basket comes out and your whiskers tell a visit is in the cards, or to kick up such a fuss when you get there that he won't be able to do anything. Nothing of the kind! Go quietly and mind your manners when you are there.

Believe it or not, most vets are the kindest men in the world and won't hurt you if they can possibly avoid it. But it won't do any good to kick up a fuss, because they are unsentimental and know almost as much about us as we do ourselves. If you make trouble, all that will happen to you is that they will wrap you in a towel or strap you down, and that is undignified and will cause you to lose face with your family.

Your first visit will be when you are very, very young, as I was, to be inoculated against distemper, for if people have all kinds of new diseases and illnesses, they also have many new ways of curing or preventing them. Inoculation is disagreeable, a prick of a needle, after which you will feel rotten for two days, but nothing fatal.

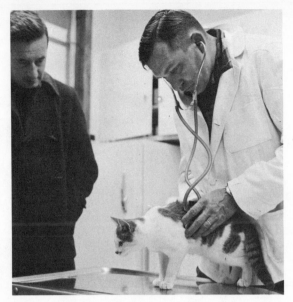

"He listens for what's wrong with you."

You will be frightened of the stinks in the place, the white table, the glaring lights, the person in the white coat whom you don't know, and the needle itself, but your own man or your woman will be there with you, and so if you have any sense, you will realize that it is all right.

And furthermore, if you are the smart cat I hope you will be, you will not let that first visit put you off so much that you will never go back or let the veterinary handle you without screaming the house down. A little too much medicine won't hurt you and is better than too little. I can tell you, I have more friends who are walking around alive today because of timely visits by, or to, the veterinary than you would believe. My man always goes with me to the vet and keeps me company.

"Ears can give you a lot of trouble . . ."   *". . . and so can teeth."*

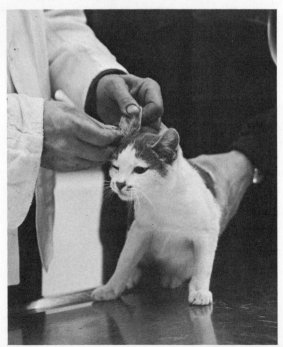

He is so crazy about me that he is inclined to be slightly hysterical if I show any symptoms that he doesn't understand, and off we go to the doctor, where he is charged ten dollars for being told that all I need, probably, is a change of diet, and this is most likely something I have been working on for days anyway. And, incidentally, you will meet a number of interesting cats and people in the waiting room, and an exciting adventure can be made out of the whole business, with your man feeling even more paternal and Godlike when it is all over.

And if you should really happen to feel ill and wretched, you will be relieved a great deal more quickly after a trip to the vet. If you are clever enough to take over a home, you will be smart enough to use your vet. A word to the wise . . .

"Believe it or not, it's for your own good."

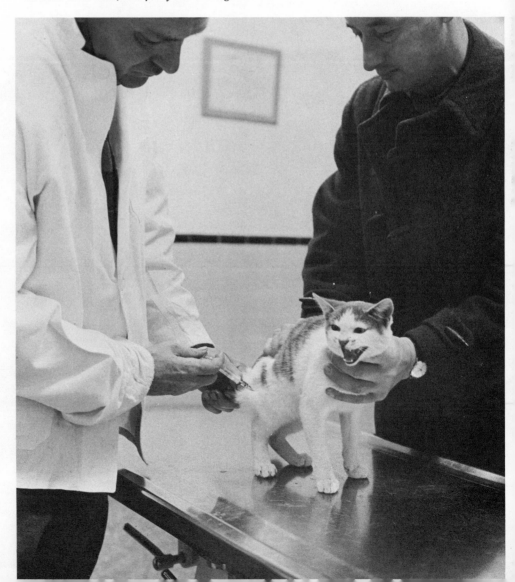

CHAPTER V

Food

WHAT DO YOU WANT? What do you like best? Crab, tinned or fresh? Fillet of Dover sole or turbot? Calves' liver, chicken livers, veal kidneys? Shad roe, salmon roe, even caviar? There is really nothing you can't have if you go about getting it in the right way. Of course, all of these things are expensive, but people have them for themselves, so why shouldn't you?

"What do you want?"

Calves' liver, for instance, is a wonderful dish until you have had chicken livers. But there is something even better, and when you have had a taste of that, you won't want chicken livers any more. It is goose livers, French imported and called *pâté de foie gras*. It comes in oval-shaped tins you can learn to recognize very quickly. It is the most expensive thing of all, next to caviar, but once you have had it you'll not care for any other kind of liver.

But don't think that you are going to get all of these delicious things just handed to you on a platter. Oh no, not a bit of it! It will be a fight for every one of them. It won't be easy, and there will be times when you are going to be pretty hungry and miserable. But if you are strong and know your people, you will win out in the end, I promise you.

Of course, you never know in the beginning under what conditions you will be feeding. They vary in practically every case according to the sort of people you may have chosen, but quite possibly you may even run up against a couple, the most difficult type, who have invested in some kind of handbook pertaining to "The Care and Feeding of Cats." But don't you worry, they can be dealt with, too. That's what *this* handbook is being written for.

If you are strong enough in character to carry out the simple rules and instructions here set down, you can achieve a most satisfactory result, so that, in the end, they will say, "Oh, well, the book must be wrong. Our cat is different." This, of course, is another portion of the pattern of our mystique, one which you must never forget. *We* are different and *you* are more different than any other.

The easiest humans with whom to cope are the ignorant, and the time to train them and make your wishes known should be at the very beginning, when they are still overcome with the honor you are doing them by remaining in their house. What is recognized by every person, simply as a piece of universal information, is that all cats like milk, and you will have no trouble on that score, unless you particularly fancy cream, in which case, using the same technique, you will educate them to giving you the top of the milk instead of having it themselves. The matter of solid food, however, is something else again, and here in their ignorance they will try everything from scrapings off their dinner plates, which are of course revolting, and you will soon cure them of *that,* to canned cat foods of various brands. There are some who will eat and relish this muck, but it need not be you.

When dealing with this ignorant class, your task is made easier since they are so pathetically eager to learn. Let us say they have put down a dish of food of some sort for you and are benignly standing by in their self-appointed roles of Givers of Good Things. Go up to it, take a good sniff or two at it, poking your nose all in and around the dish as though trying to find one single palatable article in it, per-

"Make your wishes known. . . .

Remember, many of them are ignorant. . . .

Take a good sniff or two. . . .

haps even a taste of one. Then look them full in the face for a moment. No cries of any kind are necessary; your expression will say unmistakably, "Surely you can't mean you expect me to eat this?" Walk away. Go into a corner or onto the chair you are in the process of adopting.

They will try to coax you back. Go. There is no need to be disagreeable about it. Show that you would like to be cooperative. Simply repeat the performance. You have then amply demonstrated that you would like to help them, but that it simply won't do. This ought to throw them into a preliminary panic. They may leave the dish on the chance that you are merely not hungry. You will, of course, not touch anything, and after it has been there five or six hours they will begin to worry.

At this point they may open a tin of sardines. These are not bad as an occasional change, but you wouldn't want them for a steady diet. You may indicate this by eating a half of one and then turning away. But if you are really strong-minded and anxious to establish immediately what you do like, you won't touch them. Now they will be really upset about your lack of appetite, as well as determined to solve the problem, and if they have any kind of a larder they will begin opening tins: shrimps, Japanese crab, Maine lobster tails, red caviar, liver pâté, anchovies. Select what you like and establish it as what is to be your main course with others that are acceptable. You will do the same with meats and fish, etc. How do you want it? Chopped raw? Cooked in butter? Special butcher's cuts? On the bone? Off the bone? It is up to you to let them know. By this time they will be only too grateful for your assistance.

We come now to those who know something about cat diet and the readers of those books I have already mentioned. Here you will encounter greater difficulties, and must be prepared for a showdown battle to the finish.

"Surely you don't expect me to eat this?"

Look them full in the face."

For you know and I know, and what is more, *they* know that if we are hungry enough we will eat anything and like it. Furthermore, the smart alecks who write these books will have told them that we can go without eating for long periods without showing any ill effects. Let me just quote you one of these as an example of the kind of thing you will be up against:

Never allow your cat to exercise preference in the matter of food. If it will not eat something which you know to be wholesome and good for it, then let it go without for two or three days, or even four or five if necessary, though two is usually ample to bring any cat to its senses. Once the first battle of wills has been won, you will have no further trouble.

"Simply leave it there."

I call your attention to that final sentence. It is true enough. But *you* must win that first battle.

There are various ways of accomplishing this. The simplest, of course, if you are let out, is to pick up enough nourishment at the nearest dustbin or garbage can to enable you to outlast them. Another is to eat just sufficiently to sustain you during a long campaign. Inherently, however, you are giving in if you do this, and it is bad psychology even so much as to taste the stuff.

There is a third method available, though I do not recommend this unqualifiedly, which is, after several days of refusal, to eat what they offer you and thereafter immediately throw it up onto the rug. This serves both as a criticism of their methods as well as an illustration that the food does not agree with you. However, as I say, this is not recommended. Sometimes, if the people are softhearted, it works, but if they are tough and determined and happen to be fond of their rug, you may suddenly find yourself on the wrong side of the front door, and for keeps.

The most satisfactory way, and I have rarely known it to fail, is simply to be strong enough to beat them at their own game. Refuse, refuse, refuse! Don't eat it, even if it half kills you. You lose some weight and you can pretend you are a good deal sicker than you are. For, basically, people are a lot weaker than we. Remember, we have survived absolutely unchanged over the last fifty million years or so. We were cats before anyone had ever heard of men. And there will still be cats after the last of them has blown himself off the face of the earth.

Never forget the purpose of this campaign: it is not only to defeat them on the food they have prepared for you, but to break their spirit to the point where they will being opening cans for you to taste. And the longer this duel continues, the better are your chances of winning, because you must never forget that when you are living with a man and a woman it is always a house divided, and you will have learned from earlier experience how to play one off against the other. A single man, or a single woman, naturally, will have no chance whatsoever against you in this campaign, but a married couple will support one another up to a point. That point is reached when sooner or later they will become irritated or upset for some entirely different reason and decide to use *you* to have it out. She will say: "What are you trying to do, starve that poor cat to death?" or he will begin: "You and your damn book about how to train a cat! I can't stand the way the thing looks at me any more. Either feed it or get rid of it." You then know that it is only a matter of a short time before they start reaching into the larder for something delectable, or phoning up the butcher or fishmonger.

And in the end, they will come to thank you for it, because although they do not know it, there is something else working for you in this game, and that is your snob value as an eccentric individualist for dining-out conversation, in which they are able to take part in bragging matches such as: "Our cat will eat only *moules farcie* sprinkled with cashew nuts." "Ho, ho, you think that's a funny one. Our kitty will eat nothing but Alaska king crab claws, stewed lightly in Czechoslovakian butter, served on a bed of French anchovy toast." The more complicated a dish you can work out in order that your people may come out on top in such ploys, the more grateful they will be to you in the end, and inclined to try you with new treats. Never accept anything less than total victory in this matter.

"Never accept anything less than total victory."

CHAPTER VI

Tidbits at the Table

To ACCUSTOM your people to feeding you tidbits while they are at the table calls for a direct action campaign.

At some time or another, usually in the early stages of your association, one or the other of them, but generally the man, will lay down the law to all of the others, the woman and the children, if any, with: "But no feeding at the table, understand? I won't have it!"

Don't ever make the mistake of trying to circumvent this order by playing up to the woman or one of the children. All you would do is precipitate a series of disagreeable family rows and create an atmosphere. Tackle *him* directly. Once you have broken *his* spirit and got him to slip you morsels on the sly, *then*, after you have exposed him, the rest will be easy and you will never again hear anything about the Law Against Tidbits.

Never begin by begging at once, particularly not immediately after the law has been laid down. You will only irritate him and eventually get yourself chucked out of the dining room and barred during mealtimes. No, no, pretend to acquiesce. Go over to a corner and lie down, out of the way of people serving, or pick a chair in the corner and curl up on it. The man will think that you have heard his order and are resigned to it. This serves to please him, confirm him in his role of God and lull him into a false sense of security.

"The old silent Miaow. . . ."

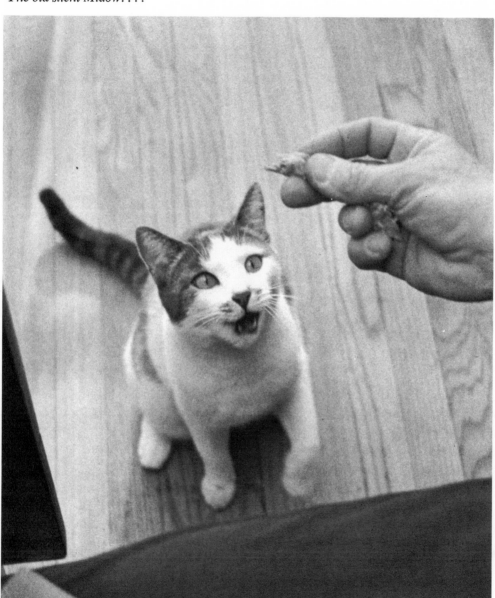

Now, one day when dinner is going well and he seems to be in a good mood, come out from your corner or get down from your chair, walk over to the table, get under it and rub your head gently against his ankles. Ten to one he will automatically reach down to pat your head or scratch your chin. It is flattering to him, and if you can manage to give a few licks to his fingers you will set him up even more for the next move.

This is where, quite quietly, so that none of the rest of the family are aware of it, you come out from under the table, sit by the side of his chair, and look up at him.

". . . the gentle shove . . ."

Do nothing as yet. He won't mind. You haven't begged, you haven't attempted to flout his authority, or break the law. You are merely being companionable, and you may even inspire that useful emotion, where he considers himself particularly favored by your attentions.

Now pick your spot, also pick your food—something specially succulent, desirable and fragrant that he is eating—and one time, when he looks down upon you fondly, give him the Silent Miaow.

There is no better opening, and once in a while it even turns the trick immediately, but if not its value lies in its silence. It doesn't alert the rest of the family to what is going on and hence there is no risk of his losing face.

Having got the message, he will know now that you would like a little of what he is having, but are not being importunate about it, and in fact, are keeping it as a little secret of communication between the two of you.

Wait. Don't hurry. More men have been lost by trying to rush them than have been gained. When you catch his eye again, give him another of the Silent Miaows and let your own fill with intense pleading, and note the reaction. If he begins talking

". . . and success is inevitable. They fall every time."

rapidly to the woman or one of his children about something irrelevant, you have registered and he has been disturbed.

Now you will be called upon to do one of the most difficult and bravest of things in your entire association. You must get up, walk away from the table, and go back to your chair. Believe me, kittens, even though you may miss out on some gorgeous snack, it is worthwhile. Besides which, they will be serving it again another day. For you will have made him feel like an absolute pig. He will have known you wanted some, it would have been in his God-given power as the Loving Father to give, and he has withheld it. Why did he withhold it? Because of the keeping of his own God-pronounced law. But who made the law? He, God. Then if he is God he can do as he pleases and unmake it. Do you begin to see the gorgeous, useful confusion you have begun to create in his mind and the insecurity that has been set in motion?

You might like to wait several days before the next move, when something particularly desirable is being served up on the table above: chicken or guinea fowl, or grouse in season (and, of course, we are assuming that you will only trouble to take over a household where they *do* serve such dishes.)

You repeat the performance, a Silent Miaow or two to get him back into the mood, and then if he hasn't reacted, reach up quietly and jog his knee or his elbow with your paw. But, for Heaven's sake, keep your claws retracted when you do. Many a good man has been lost at this stage of the game through sheer carelessness, for by sticking a needle into his leg, all you will get is a yell of, "Darn it, Kitty, don't do that! No! Get down!" But just a gentle nudge is going to keep the thing between the two of you as something grown even more intimate, and will signal, by its very gentleness, that restraint is becoming almost too much for you. How much longer can he continue to torture you thus? After all, you are such pals, he and you.

By this time, if you have brought him along properly, you can begin to look forward to, and be prepared for, success. You will see, perhaps, a furtive look come into his eyes. He will glance around the table at what the others are up to and probably begin to speak loudly, or start to abuse one of the children for the way he is eating in order to draw attention to that quarter and away from the fact that his hand has whisked a morsel from his plate and is even now sneaking down to you with the tidbit.

Should, however, the nudge fail and he proves to be of slightly stronger character, not yet prepared to surrender, then enter into the final phase of the treatment. No more Silent Miaows, no more nudges (repetition, I have already pointed out, is of no value in a campaign with people, since it only irritates). Sit there quietly at his feet, within sight, and with your eyes and head follow every movement of the fork from the plate to his mouth. Just the eyes alone won't do, my dears. You must actually *turn* your head with a kind of an upswing and a rhythm to it, of which he will very soon become aware.

I have rarely known this to fail. For what is now going on in his mind is this: Noiselessly and discreetly with the Silent Miaow, you have let him know of your need as something just between you two. Then quietly and with the same discretion, the nudge will have shown him the limit to which you were prepared to go. Now, having been rejected, you are resigned to accept your fate, but being only sub-human, you can't help your longing showing through.

One—two; one—two; onto the fork, into the mouth; the head follows, swing and up, eyes pleading. . . . The man now, if he is any kind of a man, if he ever was worth the trouble you took to domesticate him, is feeling like a complete swine—niggardly, mean-spirited, greedy, miserly—at denying someone smaller, weaker, and wholly dependent upon him something he might so easily grant. He could get out from under this unhappy, uncomfortable feeling by doing no more than—wait, watch it now! There! He has nipped something off the edge of his plate un-observed, cupped and concealed it in his hand—here it comes now, quietly closer and closer—don't be a fool and lose control at this moment and spoil everything. DON'T GRAB!

No, on the contrary! This is the moment to exercise the most exquisite caution and tact. Accept the tidbit gently and tenderly from between his fingers and retire immediately under the table with it. Don't gobble, scrunch, or smack, but put it away quietly. In this manner, even if he is regretting his momentary weakness, it will have been demonstrated that the secret is safe with you and that his breach isn't going to be punished with an immediate loss of face. He will be grateful and well disposed toward you for your cooperation.

Of course, once the initial step has been taken and he has savored the Godlike feeling of philanthropy on the q.t., he will continue to fall, each time more easily than the last, until feeling himself secure, HE will grow somewhat careless. Or, failing that, you can bring matters out into the open by taking your tidbit over to the sideboard and eating it out loud where everyone can see you. Sooner or later there will be a sudden indignant outburst from the woman: "John! Are you feeding that cat?"

But by then it will no longer matter, he will have become deep-dyed in his du-plicity, unable to break the habit, and will make some sheepish reply with a smirk, such as "I was only giving her a taste," or "She looked hungry," or "Well, it's my cat, isn't it?" and you are home. From then on *everybody* gives you tidbits.

CHAPTER VII

Attitudes

ONE OF THE MOST important things to learn for the proper and thorough subjugation of a household is attitudes. Attitudes, poses, expressions, play of body
and features, all are lumped into the manner in which you remain continually and
at all times alluring, inviting, enticing, seductive, fascinating, captivating, charming,
winning, winsome, bewitching, enchanting, engaging, interesting, prepossessing, taking, pleasing, lovely, and sweet.

I have mentioned the word "anthropomorphism" and defined its meaning in
relation to us. It is most important where attitudes are concerned, since most people
see and think of us not at all as cats, but rather as a kind of four-legged, fur-bearing
human and in some mysterious way an extension of themselves.

This is an excellent frame of mind in which to keep them, if you can. The more
they think of you as something other than you are, the less likely they will be to
pry into your secrets and discover what you are really like. Of course, you will not
stand for this business being pushed to the limit where you are considered as, and
treated like, an infant, but you can and must create the image in their minds that
you are one of the family and entitled to the same consideration as themselves, and
certainly a full cut above their servants in order of precedence. People do very well
by themselves; they deny themselves very little; they will give themselves treats more
often than not, and when one of these is going, it is important to you that you be
thought of at that moment not as a cat, but as one of them. One or another of the

"Beautiful, irresistible us!"

[74]

members of the family must be conditioned to say, "Kitty must have some, too."

They will read your expressions all wrong, but it doesn't matter. They will say, "Kitty's smiling, Kitty's laughing, Kitty's frowning, Kitty's worried, Kitty's thinking, Kitty's cross, Kitty's trying to remember something. . . ." The smile may be nothing more than opening your mouth to get a bit of air; the laugh a yawn and the frown a momentary intestinal query, but as long as they think as they do it is all to your benefit.

There is no question but that we are quite the most graceful animals in existence, and this you must keep uppermost in your mind in all of your attitudes and poses: lying down, sitting, walking, washing, sleeping, playing and hunting. The purpose of this, of course, is to hold your people consistently charmed and bemused, so that they will never for a moment stop to think of the situation between them and us in its true light, namely the extent to which we have taken over them and their homes.

People say to one another, "Keep your chin up," but I say to you, "Keep your tail up," particularly when you are walking. Don't ask me why, simply accept it as experience which has been tested, that the upraised tail when you are on promenade appears to lift the spirits of people as well.

"Everybody relax." *"Small gas pain."*

Your sleeping attitudes are as important as your waking ones, which means that you can actually continue the work of keeping your people besotted even while you are resting. The fact is, the way we sleep—either curled up in a bundle or squared with our paws tucked beneath us, or flat upon our flank with paws outstretched, or even twisted upon our backs with paws hanging limp—is relaxing to people, and when they look at us, it makes them feel good. A very effective bit is one paw over the nose or both paws over the eyes. Another to be recommended is the head resting upon one forefoot. On the back, upside down, never fails to elicit enthusiasm, particularly when on their laps.

For your waking attitudes and poses, consider your backgrounds. It isn't all catnip and cream, this taking over of a house and family, and I have never said it was, or that you don't have to do some work, or if not work then at least use the brains with which you were born. There are dozens of backgrounds against which you will look enchanting: a colored rug, a mirror, an open staircase, the branches of a tree, framed in a window, enclosed in a niche, against a cushion, on a mantelpiece, amongst ornaments, on a fur coat of a contrasting shade, or in a doorway. It is up to you to learn them, find them, and make use of them.

"Laughing? Nonsense! It's a yawn."

"Two of me is better than one."

Never, never, NEVER let yourself be caught in an awkward or undignified pose, so that you are likely to be laughed at. Believe me, it takes days to recover control again, if ever you have been the subject of laughter. You may amuse them so that they laugh with you, but never at you. This means you must always be in complete control of your body and its attitudes. Never attempt to jump up unless you are one hundred per cent sure of making it, lest you fall back and nearly break your spine twisting around to keep up the fiction that we always land on our feet. Never become involved in anything that you have not thoroughly tested out beforehand. For if you make yourself ridiculous, in a way you are making *them* ridiculous.

All of you, of course, are familiar with the difference between the wash for hygiene and the wash for effect. There is no need to be self-conscious about your after-meal cleanup; it will be expected of you and you can be as thorough as you like without having to worry too much how you look. However, your washes to call attention to yourself, to change the subject, to get out of an embarrassing situation or to indicate or punctuate your feelings, must be nicely calculated and prettily posed, and here I recommend the sitting-up position with the head turned slightly, an expression of extreme concentration on your face as you give your shoulder a few sweeping licks. It is a most graceful and compelling movement, and will always hold an audience.

Another highly effective company wash is to lie down on a rug in the middle of the room, full length, and do the over-the-shoulder movement. It won't take more than four or five licks before everyone will be looking at you, and what is more, talking about you. If there are guests present they will begin telling about their own cat, which will lead your people to try to top them, and in doing so, exercise their imaginations. The more of this you can induce the better, since eventually they will come to believe their own stories.

You need never worry about your attitudes during play or even when stalking a mouse or a shrew in the fields, or tossing a dead one about, for at these times—in fact practically always—you are so naturally graceful that you cannot fail to charm them. They will sometimes indulge you for hours in this manner with a catnip mouse or a bit of paper tied to the end of a string, which they will either drag along the floor or swing in the air above your head for you to leap up and catch with your paws.

Graceful

Acrobatic   *Dainty*

033 825 1033 829 1033 83

826 830 83

827 831 835

828 832 836

"Unself-conscious—and magnificent."

"You need never worry about your attitudes when stalking—every one of them will be exquisite."

And speaking of this, as you will learn, they often enjoy taking photographs of you. Some of these have managed to catch us in mid-air, and you will be both surprised and pleased to see how very attractive you look under those circumstances. If ever you find you are given the opportunity to examine a set of these pictures, do so, not only for the purpose of noting any mistake you may have made, but for the sheer pleasure you will derive from seeing how perfectly you are able to maintain your form and technique while off the ground.

When considering your attitudes and their effect upon your people it is most important for you to know that when you are young and still considered kittens, you are permitted to assume every kind of position and get into all sorts of trouble

"Superb . . .   *gorgeous . . .*

or absurd situations with no loss of dignity. They will only remark that you are "cute," a word they will often apply to you and which you will eventually outgrow, and you need never mind their laughing at you then, for what you are actually doing is stealing your way into their hearts and solidifying your position. Thus you may crawl into the pigeonholes of a desk, fall into the flour bin, tumble into wastebaskets, sprawl out of cardboard boxes, topple from chairs, climb up screen doors, get entangled in electric wires or balls of yarn, slip off the bed, skid on a polished floor, get yourself all wrapped up in paper or knock over a flower vase. You are not to worry if you break anything, or spill water, or get yourself covered with flour, ink, or paint. They won't be able to be angry with you and you will soon learn

enchanting . . .   *Me!"*

which of your youthful pranks please them the most.

I had thought at first to make a separate section under gestures, but it seems to me that the few there are may well be classified with attitudes. These are things that you will do actively, rather than assume a pose to convey a message or merely to enhance the image they have of you.

Cruising back and forth through their ankles, tail in the air, pushing up against them, for instance, will be one of these, and is useful when they are preparing your food to show them how interested and pleased and excited you are at the prospect. It appeals to their vanity as the God-givers of things to small, (so-called) helpless creatures and may get you special care in the preparation of your dish, larger portions and nicer tidbits.

"The gesture they can't resist."

When you bestow a lick or two upon a hand or cheek it enthralls them, since they don't know your reason for this is that the salt on their skin is sometimes not unpleasant. *They* think and say that you are kissing them, which is something their males and females seem to like to do to one another. Well, an occasional lick won't hurt you and it is tremendously effective. So is the use of your paws. For some reason I have never been able to understand or explain, they *love* to have you put your feet in their faces. And if you can manage to hold their cheeks, chins, or noses in your front paws for a moment or two, or curl one or the other or both your front legs about their necks, they will go into absolute transports of delight, especially if you will learn to rub your head against their cheeks and purr a little. In this you will only be scratching and pleasuring yourself, but *they* accept it as a demonstration of exclusive affection for them and feel themselves practically engaged to you.

But if you really ever wish to make a gesture which will turn them inside out with joy and consolidate your position, present them with a dead mouse.

They will carry on as though you had given them a mansion, a million dollars, a Rolls-Royce, and a mink coat for the lady of the house. They will call up their friends on the telephone and tell them, talk about it at dinner parties, and write letters to the newspapers.

It has become pretty difficult for a city cat to find a decent mouse, what with modern sanitary engineering and apartment houses, but if you happen to live in the country, don't fail to avail yourself of this gambit.

Do not ask me why this has such a tremendous effect upon people. Probably it has something to do with the legend that we like to eat mice, and are making a supreme sacrifice by presenting them with our supper. We happen to know that mouse-catching is pure sport, and that unless we were starving we wouldn't any more taste one than they would eat a fox after they had run it down. The point is they won't know the difference if it happens to be a used-up mouse, with which you had been playing, that you give them. Any mouse, any time, bowls them over.

CHAPTER VIII

Doors

DOORS ARE A PROBLEM in any house you will ever live in, and you simply have to learn to cope with them, or rather, with your people, and teach them the necessity of dropping whatever they happen to be doing to open one of them to let you in or out.

If you are fortunate you will have taken over a family both sufficiently cat-minded as well as ingenious to rig up one of those patent affairs cut into the bottom of the front door, which enables us to come and go as we please.

This, of course, is ideal for everyone, particularly for us, and enables us to get out at night without a lot of questions or admonitions. However, this does not solve the problem of inside doors, the ones to rooms, closets, cupboards, cellars, attics, etc., and the rule that you must try to establish at your earliest possible opportunity is that they must be *left open at all times*. You may have some difficulty with those leading from one room into another, or connecting with hallways, since the male of the family will be shouting about draughts, but there is no reason whatsoever why closet or cupboard doors should be kept shut.

You can learn very quickly how to open a door yourself, particularly if it is of the bent-handle kind, which you can work merely by getting up on your hind legs and putting your weight upon it. The round, doorknob handle is somewhat more of a problem, but when you have your full growth and weight you will find that by pushing or pulling on it you can get it to turn sufficiently to slip the latch.

"You can learn how to open a door yourself."

"You may suddenly find yourself shut into a closet."

However, when you have learned these tricks, don't, under any circumstances, let your family know that you have. It is their business and absolute concern to open and shut doors for you at any time, and your own little skill you will keep to yourself, for use at such times as when you may suddenly find yourself shut in a cupboard or when, for some reason or other, you are forbidden to go out.

To come in from the outside, scratching on the door and a good, loud miaow will alert someone. For an inside job, if your people are properly conditioned, it will be necessary to do no more than to go and sit by the door and just look at it. If that doesn't work pretty soon, you turn and look at them. If they are busy doing something give your miaow that they have come to connect with impatience. Whichever, remember that once you have attracted their attention to the fact that you want to get out, never let them go back to what they were doing. In any well-regulated household you come first.

"Out!" *"In!"*

CHAPTER IX

Christmas

CHRISTMAS IS AN ANNUAL family celebration amongst people, at which time presents are exchanged and enormous quantities of food are eaten. Also a fir tree is brought into the house and decorated by hanging a number of glittering objects upon it. With a little determination and firmness you can very easily make this *your* celebration for *your* benefit and run the way *you* want it. It is not at all extraordinary on Christmas Eve or Christmas Day to hear the mother or the father say to the children, "We can't open the packages yet; Kitty isn't here." This is a well-trained family.

For opening the parcels is the most gorgeous fun for us, since they all come wrapped in the most rustly kind of tissue paper and are tied up with colored ribbons. As they are unwrapped we can roll in the tissue paper, use it for ambushes, shred it to bits, and play with the ribbons. Certain things will come packed in cardboard boxes, into which we can get immediately, and if we want to do so, stake out a permanent claim. Irrespective of special presents for us in the shape of catnip mice, ping-pong balls, or other toys, we can also sniff into and play with everybody else's presents.

Christmas is a gluttonous time for people. It certainly has been in every family I have ever known. It should also be for us, and doubly so, since we can get in both during the preparation of things as well as the final eating of them. For instance, there will be a taste of the turkey stuffing to cadge, or snippets of liver and lights which the mistress of the house will slip you if the Christmas spirit is upon her.

"You can very easily make Christmas your celebration."

"Naturally, these were made for me`..."

And with regard to this Christmas spirit, you should be aware that during this time an extra feeling of kindliness is present in all members of the family, and you can very often get away with things that otherwise might not be tolerated, no matter how well you have trained your people.

It is, of course, unthinkable at the dinner table that they have turkey and you don't share. Make certain that you get some. It is your right. A word to the wise: don't overeat and then throw up on the rug. It will just make you unpopular and spoil what is otherwise a most enjoyable day. At the finish of the meal there is a highly indigestible concoction called plum pudding, which I would strongly advise you not to touch.

But the greatest delight of Christmas, put up for your edification, is the tree, with its many bright ornaments, a number of them hung within batting distance. Reach up with your paw and hit them and they will swing to and fro most excitingly, calling for more bats and eventually a grab. There is tinsel, too, sagging invitingly; cornucopias, peppermint sticks, glass birds, and every kind of interesting article, as though the makers had sat up nights working out what would be most appealing to cats and kittens. In order to catch the light attractively, most of these objects are made of the thinnest kind of glass, and break very easily, but don't worry; there

[91]

"... and it's my right to play with them...."

"Plenty more where those came from."

are always plenty more where they came from. You are entitled then to play with this tree and everything on it to your heart's content, and even get up into it, if it is big enough and you feel like it. It makes for a most interesting and important attitude, provided you don't knock the tree over, which will cause a bit of a rumpus. If, in the course of playing with an ornament you should catch a claw in a branch and pull the tree down, simply go and hide under the couch until someone comes and rights it. Never forget, that noncommunication is the tenth point of the law. If nobody saw you do it, you can't be interrogated and so are not even called upon to lie. They may suspect you but they can't prove it.

The Christmas spirit may last from about the twenty-third of December to the twenty-seventh, sometimes to the New Year, but never make the mistake of counting upon finding any remaining traces of it after that. In particular, if you are wise, you will refrain from irritating the male member of the family for several weeks thereafter. This is when the bills come in.

A Happy Christmas to you all who have never before encountered this thrilling and delectable festival.

"Wrapping paper is the most fun."

CHAPTER X

Traveling

A WORD ABOUT TRIPS. If you have succeeded properly in putting your family under obligation to you, they will not want to leave you behind when they go for a ride, particularly if you have managed to display some of the good manners I have referred to in an earlier chapter. Now there are a number of methods of transportation—steamship, railroad train, airplane—some of which, when it comes to noise and

"Nobody's kidding me."

stinks, are pretty terrifying. Even though you know that you are going along on the trip, your tendency will be to struggle against being placed in the traveling cat-box, since all of us are prone to claustrophobia and cannot bear to be confined in small places. If you are intelligent you will control this phobia and welcome the safety for the journey, remembering that it is your protection. If you are unable to get out, neither can anything else get in. You will be as safe as a mouse in its hole, even if you have to ride in the baggage compartment for a time; nobody can touch you with dirty hands or mess you about. It is worth it not to be left behind. Whatever they wish you to use, cat-box, wicker basket, small handbag, acquiesce. This is not the place to exert your authority.

"I've conned her into letting me ride front seat."

Remember, when traveling people have to obey all kinds of rules and regulations that they don't make themselves. If you want to go, go quietly.

On the other hand, when it comes to accompanying them in their motorcars, if you can con them into letting you ride in the back seat (and it is very easy to accustom them to this; simply don't get hysterical the first time they take you, and if it is a long ride and they let you out for you-know-what, remember, *that* is not the time to play games and disappear) you will have the most glorious view of everything that is going on. You can even learn to lie quietly across the shoulders of the driver or another passenger, which makes for comfort and companionship. It is the most delightful way ever invented for traveling.

"I could drive it if I felt like it."

"I encountered a pure white tomcat . . ."

CHAPTER XI

Motherhood

MOTHERHOOD IS the most wonderful thing in the world. I have had my kittens and wouldn't have missed the fun for anything. I am all for it, and you won't catch me talking against maternity, provided someone else, not me, has the next batch and the fuss and trouble of bringing them up and having homes found for them.

". . . and fell madly in love with him . . ."

". . . the things he said to me . . ."

Of course there have to be kittens, otherwise there wouldn't be any more cats, but there are plenty of others who like to spend their time producing them, and I say leave it to them. It is not for me, or for you either, if you want to be a boss cat and run a human family the way they should be, for your own comfort and well-being.

Kittens can happen to anyone, and should it occur to you who have read and absorbed this manual, you may take it as a Horus-sent opportunity to inculcate what you have learned from this book into your offspring, who in turn will teach it to theirs and thus increase our sway over the human race to the point where we will eventually attain the eminence we deserve as rulers of the earth.

However, there is also your position as house cat supreme to be considered. You have things going along nicely the way you want them, everything routined properly for your benefit, your humans lulled and content with their lot. All at once you upset it by producing a handful of tiny, helpless creatures.

". . . one thing led to another."

Humans dislike nothing so much as having the order of their lives broken into or altered, and believe me, a batch of kittens calls for changes. And suddenly your people are aware of your existence; they must walk carefully for fear of stepping on something soft and furry that has got under their feet; they can no longer sit down upon a chair without first looking; and homes must eventually be found for the newcomers. The imminence of birth gives them qualms—humans make a tremendous fuss about this simple procedure; children, if any, begin asking questions; there is usually one weak sister-kitten that has to be fed from a medicine-dropper; beds and boxes have to be shifted about to warm places, and all in all there is considerable disruption and hullabaloo and *you* are the one who has done it. In their fervor to

"And this is what you get—number one."

"Four! You'd be exhausted, too."

"I suppose you've noticed. One is the image of his father."

place the kittens in adequate homes, they might just suddenly wonder what life would be like without any cat at all about the house. Once you get them thinking that, you could be halfway out the door.

Mind you, I am not saying don't have kittens, I'm just saying reflect; think it over; consider your family, their household, their status, etc. It just so happened that my people enjoy trouble and had an absolute field-day with my *accouchement* and delivery. It was not until later that certain difficulties began to make themselves manifest.

It all happened to me a long time ago, when I was very young, and of course I wasn't as fortunate as you are in having such a handbook as this to guide me. I had my man and his wife nicely subjugated, the house running smoothly and peacefully my way when I fell in love with never a thought to the consequences.

He was pure white, a veritable White Knight, I tell you, and an absolutely fascinating devil. I lost my head. The things he told me and the promises he made! I was this; I was that; I was unique; I was the center of his universe.

"From then on my life wasn't my own—"

"Snatch a meal when you can. . . ."

"People poking their noses in . . ."

I have always known that I was unique and certainly I was the center of the world of my people. But you know, it's different when you hear someone else say it. I listened to him. We went for long walks together outdoors. He became more and more persuasive. One thing led to another, and one day . . .

I was a good mother. I was probably the best mother that ever was, else how would I be able to write this book of maxims for the young? In fact, thanks to the education I was able to give them, every one of my kittens has made a great success, and each one has his, or her, family properly reduced and subservient. And I'm proud of them.

I even enjoyed having them, including mother love and all the worries and idiocies connected with the whole business. I am sure I made a charming picture with my brood about me, nursing or cuddled close, but that doesn't alter the fact that they were also a great nuisance at times and nearly resulted in breaking up our formerly quiet, happy household.

"Shifting them about."

"And posing for the announcement: 'Madonna and Kittens.' Ha! Ha!"

"So then you get a lot of children handling them . . ."

Just as one example of what can happen, the man became insanely jealous of me because of the attention I, as an American mother, would naturally wish to lavish upon my kittens. Whenever *he* wanted to play with me I was busy washing them, or feeding them, or carrying them from one place to another to get them out of harm's way. And before long he was making himself unpleasant to his wife as well, because she was paying too much attention to the kittens and cooing over them, and he started to grumble about his house being turned into a cattery.

Well, and then later on when the kittens had grown big enough to play around and crawl up his legs and chase after him, *my* nose was put out of joint by the fact that he began to make more fuss over the kittens than he did over me, and that didn't make for harmonious relations.

I have already covered the subject of the charm of kittens in my chapter on attitudes, and as I said before, I am sure no cat looked more inspirational or bewitching than I, feeding my brood or surrounded by them tumbling over me, but that didn't alter the fact that we were suddenly five where before there was only one and that one was *me*.

And don't forget that in the beginning it is *you* who are feeding them and no extra expense to anyone. Then the day comes when they are weaned and another dish of food has to appear. Up goes the milk bill at the end of the month. You think the man doesn't notice that?

". . . and deciding which one to adopt."

And then, just as you are starting to make some headway with their education and knocking some sense into them, the question of homes for them arises again and once more your household is upset. For it isn't so easy to find satisfactory candidates for four or five kittens all at one time because, as you will have gathered from the whole tenor of this book, the average person really does not know that he wants a cat at all. He must be *made* to realize it—in other words, taken over. Well, a clever cat can do this, but remember, even if you have taught your kittens properly they are still inexperienced, and when people try to press cats on others there is always considerably increased suspicion and resistance on the part of the pressees.

"But in the meantime I've got to keep an eye on them."

"On the go from morning until night."

Therefore, children who are pushovers when it comes to kittens have to be found, which means that during this time the house is cluttered up with small fry of all kinds and ages being exposed to them. Muddy feet are dirtying up the carpets and upsetting the furniture. I don't like my youngsters, before their bones are formed, handled by some idiot child who might squeeze the life out of them, so that I am in a panic constantly; usually there is a row when two of the children want the same kitten, or

"You just try keeping track of four all at once."

there's one left over that nobody seems to care about, and then the family gets edgy and, of course, you are to blame.

That's when the idea is likely to come to them that as long as they are cleaning out a batch of kittens and finding homes, why not do a hundred per cent job and get rid of you too, and start all over again with some peace in the house.

For you must know that at this point they will be faced with one or two alternatives. You will either continue to have litters of kittens, with the same procedure all over again, only less friends remaining who are willing to take them. Or there will have to be an expensive and dangerous operation so that you will not be able to have any more. Either way calls for a decision, and humans simply can't bear to make decisions. There is a third way out, as I have said, which would be to get rid of you. I don't say it will always happen, but a smart cat plays the percentages. Next time that White Knight shows up at the door, go get your catnip mouse, start playing with it, and forget about him.

"And the older they get, the more nuisance they are . . ."

". . . unless they're sleeping . . ."

". . . or stuffing themselves."

"One of the kittens is always . . ."　　　　*". . . more adventurous than the others . . ."*

". . . than keep an eye on her . . ."　　*". . . Work! Work! Work!"*　　*"Come back here, you little——. . ."*

". . . which means more work for mother."

". . . thinks I have nothing better to do . . ."

". . . always getting under my feet . . ."

CHAPTER XII

Speech

The Silent Miaow

I CANNOT BEGIN to tell you how effective the Silent Miaow can be for breaking down resistance, always provided you don't overdo it but save it for the right moment.

The technique for this is ridiculously simple. You look up at the subject, open your mouth as you would for a fully articulated miaow, such as you emit if, say, you wish to leave the room and want the door opened, or are hungry or irritated by something, except in this case you permit no sound to issue.

The effect is simply staggering. The man or the woman appears to be shaken to the core, and will give you practically anything, which is why I say you must not use it often, for one of the human traits, in fact reduced to a proverb, is that "Familiarity breeds contempt." Whereas in our world, as you know, the proverb reads, "Familiarity breeds contentment."

Even I, who have made a lifelong study of the human species, am not able to tell you exactly why the Silent Miaow has this devastating effect, or even the exact emotion it inspires in people. The nearest I can come to it is that it creates a picture of helplessness that the God syndrome is unable to resist. We are already fortunate that certain notes of our spoken language, the miaow, resemble the cries of their own infants, the sound with which their young communicate their need for food, warmth, attention, or whatever it is they may be lacking. People have become conditioned to immediate response to this baby-wauling and thus, by association, a similar desire to do something about it can be evoked by the properly placed and pitiful miaow.

People, it seems, communicate principally vocally, and their clacking and chattering goes on interminably from morn till night and, believe it or not, some of them even continue to talk in their sleep.

"Practice the Silent Miaow right from the beginning."

Thus they will always think of the sounds we make in terms of theirs, and think of our language as being like theirs which, of course, could not possibly be wider of the mark.

To return, then, to the Silent Miaow. It appears to sum up for them such a burden of unhappiness and need that we are not able even to give voice to it. It is an un-cry of despair and longing that pierces more swiftly and directly to the human heart than the most self-pitying miaow of which we are capable and, I suspect, corresponds in the human mind to their own facial expressions of love, despair, anguish or entreaty, with which they are in the habit of supplementing their speech.

Speaking for myself, I usually confine the use of the Silent Miaow to begging at the dinner table, as indicated in my writing upon that subject, but it can also be used to good effect at other times when you want something you feel they are not inclined to give you.

The Active Miaow

I have referred in the above section to the pitiful miaow as among the most effective sounds you can produce to get some action out of your people, and to this must be added the sound that all of you will know how to produce, which has a most remarkable softening-up effect; it is that little lilt of ours, a chirrup, which goes, "Prrrr-maow," with a rising inflection upon the last syllable. This sound of ours has no specific use vis-à-vis people; except that for some reason or other it just seems to make them feel fine, and puts them into a good humor. We use it naturally from time to time as a kind of a greeting, or when we are in a particularly benign mood, and also when we happen to be carrying kittens, and I simply call it to your attention as yet another item in the armory for keeping our people in a state of subjugation and prepared to wait on us.

Fortunately for us, they are not all unintelligent, in a way, and you will find that it will not take you long to teach them various sounds you make, that is to say certain kinds of miaow, and what you mean by them. As you know, we, of course, have entirely different methods of communicating with one another in our world, but people are mostly dependent upon what they can hear, and hence this is what you use.

For instance, if you will go over and sit by the door and do a kind of short, scratchy miaow and perhaps even touch the door with your paw until they let you out, you will find that after a time your people are able to make the connection between that kind of a miaow and the fact that you want the door opened for you. You can do the same for food, or wanting your toys, or "Get-off-my-chair," until you have taught them quite a useful little vocabulary of eight or ten sounds, certainly all you need for *your* purposes, for you obviously won't wish to become any further involved in talk with them. For, and this is only an anthropological sideline upon the species, you will notice after you have lived with them for a long time that it is their constant talk and chatter that seems to land them in most of the trouble into which they get themselves. Remember, it does not matter which sounds or miaows you use for this reason, so long as each time you use the *same* one for each purpose. You can invent your own language here, and it is rather a good idea to do so, instead of copying that of some other cat, for here again you convey the desired illusion of exclusiveness, a secret means of communication between your people and yourself that cannot be understood by anyone else and will enable them to boast, "When our cat wants to go out she goes like this: '———.' I never heard any other cat do that."

"The effect is simply staggering."   *"Here it is—the un-cry of despair."*

The Purr

You might think that the purr should be included above in the general catalogue of sounds we use to make our wants known, but actually I have always felt that this noise remains in a class of its own in its use and effect upon humans.

To begin with, it is a mystery. No one has ever been able to discover how we make this subtle sound, and what is more, no one ever will. It is a secret that has endured from the very beginning of the time of cats and will never be revealed.

We purr naturally under the stimulus of various shades and grades of contentment, but it is only since we have domesticated man to our use and purposes that we have come to understand its effect upon humans.

Were it not for one pronounced and never absent trait of human beings, their vanity, our problems vis-à-vis them would be so much greater and complicated than they are. For if you are reading this handbook carefully, or if as an old, established house cat you have made your own observations, you must, if you have any intelligence, have come to the conclusion that the greater part of our success in achieving our ends is based upon human vanity and the weaknesses to which it exposes our people.

"The purr in spite of oneself."

"*You don't purr at this kind of treatment.*"   "*You do for this.*"

The purr is no exception to this rule. And since on one level man has self-appointed himself as God in connection with us, the purr is considered and accepted as a prayer of thanks. Thanks, in the human relationship, is a powerful form of flattery. Man's own God, who Himself appears to thrive upon flattery of the most obsequious kind, is always being thanked.

Thus if a man strokes you and you begin to purr, the implication is immediate. He has made you so happy that you are unable to contain your gratitude.

Purrs fall into two classes: the first, the Post-Appreciative or Thankful Purr, and the second, the Anticipatory Purr.

The Anticipatory Purr is a powerful stimulant if you want some action, and when combined so as to follow immediately upon the Silent Miaow, is practically irresistible.

Since the purr is accepted in every country of the world as indicative that you have been pleasured, the Anticipatory Purr is most useful in jogging the conscience of a human and making him or her feel guilty if he fails to come through. An advance purr at mealtimes or when cadging, or if they are packing up to go for a day in the country and you'd like to go along too, makes it almost impossible for them to refuse to gratify what you are already thanking them for.

As for the Post-Appreciative Purr, the times and places of its uses are too numerous to mention, but the effect is always the same. Your person is aware that you are grateful for something *he* or *she* has done for you, or is doing. A purr is appropriate after your dish of food has been set down (always providing, as covered in Chapter V, it is to your liking); when you have curled into your favorite chair; when you have got up onto the bed; when you have settled down before the fire and it is obvious no one is going to bother you; when you are being stroked languorously and properly, or when a particularly luscious tidbit has been sneaked to you. Upon each occasion your contentment will be transferred to engage the vanity and aggrandize the donor of whatever it is that has caused your manifestation of satisfaction.

You may range from the barely perceptible purr, which leaves one not quite certain whether or not one has managed to placate you, to the thunderous one, which can be heard halfway across the room.

There is also an important adjunct to this, namely the Withheld Purr, which is highly effective if your people have transgressed and you are engaged in letting them know that they have, and punishing them.

For instance, when your man, with whom you are justifiably angry because he refused to share his breakfast bacon with you that morning, or ignored you altogether, comes home at night and fetches you up off the floor onto his lap, strokes you, and gives you your favorite kind of scratching or tickling under the chin, which ordinarily would lead you to produce a powerful purr, you don't. You do nothing. You sit on his knee like a bump on a log. You don't dig your claws into his flesh or try to escape, you just don't purr. At first he won't know what is troubling him; he will just feel that something isn't as it should be somewhere and he will try to remember whether it was anything that happened at the office or perhaps something not quite right at home, like his beloved pipe missing or a picture hanging crookedly. Eventually he will narrow it down and realize that it is you. Your esophagus ought to be throbbing but it is not. He will then ask you what the matter is, and redouble his efforts, stroking, scratching, loving, cajoling. And you still won't purr. By this time he will get the message and realize that he is being put into Coventry, or, as the slang phrase goes, "in the Dog House." This will cause him to feel guilty, as indeed he should, and the guilty feeling will make him pettish and snappish with his wife and children at the dinner table; *they* will turn upon him as a result and likewise consign him to the Dog House, which is exactly the effect that you wish to achieve by withholding the purr.

CHAPTER XIII

Manners

WE ARE ALL in agreement on the many benefits we bestow upon humans and how fortunate they are when we decide to take one or more of them over and accept their way of living, but I should be derelict in my duty if I did not point out the necessity for good manners and proper behavior in one's relationship with them.

We must admit and face the unfortunate fact that there are many cats so conceited and arrogant that they give nothing whatsoever to the people with whom they live and, in fact, delight in abusing, mistreating, and scorning them, always out of sorts and disagreeable and never yielding an inch of themselves. The astonishing thing is that there are people who actually *enjoy* this kind of treatment, and some who demand it or ask for it. They even take a curious pride in having a disagreeable cat, but of course these are exceptions.

Two of the problems confronting you will be when to let yourself be picked up, and when to remain upon a lap and when not. Theoretically, if you have done your preliminary work well, the understanding will be that you *never* stay on laps if you don't wish to do so, *never* come in from the outside when called, never, in fact, do anything that you do not wish to do, for if you did you would destroy the image of the independent cat, which down through the ages has been so great a part of our success. Remember, this is the legend we have created and kept alive for thousands of years, to the point where it may be safely considered that we are the most free and important creatures in the world.

Good manners, however, call for a knowledge of when to set aside or ignore what we know to be our rights, and behave gracefully without in any way diminishing our authority.

Returning to the pick-up. To begin with, you don't count being picked up by children. If you select a house where there is a child, or one should appear after you have moved in and you don't move out, well then, being picked up at all hours in all kinds of uncomfortable ways and lugged about is part of it. The well-mannered cat will not struggle or complain and may even get to enjoy it after a while.

Now, as to the person who picks you up and plonks you onto his or her lap when you have other things on your mind, or are busy with your own thoughts and don't wish to be on a lap and *don't* want to be scratched and are not at all in the mood to have a heavy hand passed over your fur, the cat who has been properly brought up will evaluate the reason why it is being lapped, and after you have had some experience with humans you will always know.

Are they showing off? Are they worried about something? Are they bloody-minded? Very often they are bothered over something and do it only because they

A time to remember manners

know it annoys you. In that case, of course, and in unmistakable terms, you excuse yourself.

But there are moments when your human will be sad, hurt, lonely, depressed and will actually need you to hold and to touch and in some way to be reassured, and this, I say, you will learn to feel. Good manners call for you to submit at this point, to relax upon the lap, and if you can manage it, to bestow a lick or two upon the hand.

As to coming when called, the greater part of our picture of independence is that of all the animals we never, never, never come when called. Dogs do, horses do, even sheep, cows, pigs and chickens can be taught to, but we don't. Yet there are times when proper manners call upon you to do just that, and one of them is, let us say, when your man and woman are entertaining guests and your man summons you. Whether you are in or out of the room you should go to him at once. The point is you never let your people down in front of company, irrespective of the fact that this show of politeness will so set up your man, both in the eyes of the guests and in his own estimation, that for days thereafter you will be able to get anything you like out of him.

In the same manner you will be able to cooperate with your family in the entertainment of an important guest who likes cats and happens to take a fancy to you. Again experience will teach you just how VIP a guest is, and how much depends upon the visit, both from what your people say and their attitude toward the visitor. When the latter picks you up and takes you onto his lap, stay there and make a fuss over him. More fat contracts have been landed and promotions granted because a member of the family was able to say, "My goodness, I have never seen Kitty take to anyone like that. She must know that you are really a wonderful person."

Afterwards you may hear your family say, "Golly! What a good thing that Kitty didn't dig her claws into old J.G.'s knee and spit in his eye, as she usually does with guests. I wonder what got into her?" Nothing, of course, but the sheer good manners I would expect of any kitten I ever taught, and putting your best foot forward where you can do something for your people.

Of course, as soon as the company has gone and things return to normal, so may you. When someone calls you, certainly don't come, and if you are picked up against your will, it is your right to get away in any fashion you can, and if afterwards there is a call for iodine and band-aid, well, *you* didn't start it. Spoiling never did anyone any good.

The well-behaved cat doesn't get up onto the dining-room table or the kitchen table. If you have broken in your family properly where your food is concerned, you won't have to. Stealing is for dogs. We are above it.

The same goes for begging at the table. In my chapter on tibdits I have taught you how to make an arrangement between yourself and your man, or your woman. Making a fuss at the tableside and digging your spikes into people's legs in an attempt to panhandle a bit of food detracts from your dignity.

If your family has provided you with a scratching post, or you live in the country and are allowed to go out frequently where there are trees, it is the worst possible manners to sharpen your claws on the damask of the Louis XV drawing-room chair. Besides which, it will get you into trouble, and if there should happen to be any kind of a campaign on by a member of your family to get rid of you, you will find that you have added a good deal of fuel to the fire. If statistics were available they would show that more cats have been chucked for exercising their claws on the furniture than for any other cause. Today, a scratching post is a recognized adjunct in any city household that lives with a cat.

"Coming in when called flatters them like nothing else."

Still, there are some people, and it takes all kinds to make up their world, too, who simply don't know, and here it is permissible to hint at what you want by taking a gouge or two out of the sofa or the bedpost. In nine cases out of ten, very shortly thereafter you will have a scratching post. In the tenth case, well, obviously you haven't chosen very bright people, and whether you are chucked or not oughn't to matter too much.

Whilst the subject is still open to controversy, I am of the generation that believes that submission to grooming is not part of good manners and comes rather under the head of personal conviction. We are perfectly capable of looking after our own coats, and have indeed done so for centuries, even when living out in the wilds. Granted, it is a convenience to be de-ticked or to have burrs removed from one's fur, and a well-mannered cat will remain still during this process and not make

"The sooner you learn to use this, the less trouble you will have . . ."   *". . . or do it outdoors."*

"From the very beginning we are capable of looking after ourselves . . ."

". . . at either end."

"We don't have to put up with this sort of thing . . ."

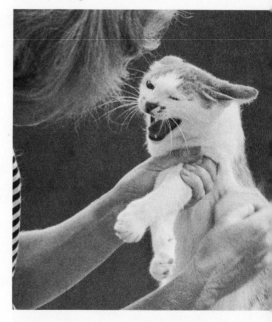

". . . or this."

things more difficult. But I cannot hold with this eternal game of brushing with shell, steel, or bristles, which people are always having to do to themselves to keep looking presentable and hence feel that they have to do to us. If you enjoy being stroked with a brush, and if·properly done it can be very pleasurable, well and good. But if you don't, I see no reason why you should stand for it. The simplest way out when you see them going for the brush is to run and hide so they can't find you, and eventually they will have something else to do. But if you are fairly caught, you may, as far as I am concerned, use any method you like to avoid this kind of treatment. One very effective measure of registering your protest is, immediately after they have had their way with you and get that smug, satisfied look upon their faces, to go at once and roll in something, the dirtier the better.

Finally, a word on guests and behavior. Quite a few of them very often will bring their dogs into the house. Whatever your feelings may be on the subject of these disgusting creatures, good manners call for you to ignore the brute. Get up onto the piano or the sideboard, turn your back, and stay there until he has gone.

CHAPTER XIV

Love

LOVE IS A DIFFICULT and delicate subject. It is a feeling that comes stealing over you sometimes, and until you have experienced it you may not understand what I am saying, and must therefore take my word for it. I refer, of course, to love of people.

For, in spite of everything I have written with the aim of making easier your task of securing a comfortable home and taking over the people who will occupy it with you, love is the unknown factor that, in nine out of ten cases, you will find will enter into the relationship. It is a mysterious thing that no one has ever been able to find the location or the cause of, something like our purr. It is not at all like the instinct that sends us out looking for a husband. Oh, no! It is something quite different and most difficult to explain, except that when it happens to you, you will know it. It has happened to me with the family with which I have lived since I took them over as a very young kitten, as I have narrated in the beginning of this book. I love them and they love me. There! I have said it! And I am not ashamed of it.

You cannot live for any length of time with humans without learning that, in addition to a few good qualities, they are stupid, vain, stubborn, forgetful, often sly and false. They tell outright lies; they say one thing and mean quite another; they make promises that they break, and are often selfish, greedy, inconsiderate, possessive and inconsistent, cowardly, jealous, irresponsible, autocratic, intolerant, impatient, hypocritical, and slovenly. Yet with all these handicaps they have this strong and wonderful thing they call love, and when they love you and *you* love them, none

"Love is a difficult and delicate subject."

of the other things seem to matter, though of course—a word of caution here—you must never lose your head so completely as to fail to protect yourself in accordance with the ways and means I have set down in this volume.

Although you will never solve the mystery of this human love, you will no doubt discover, as I did, something that is a part of it, a characteristic of every person—male or female, young or old, good or bad—you will ever encounter, without exception. They are all lonely, but unlike us, are not self-sufficient enough to bear it as we can. And perhaps what lies at the bottom of the power we are able to wield over them is the fact *that they need us* to help them in this state. And while I may have been seemingly harsh and cruel in my attitude toward them for *your* protection, when I think about my family and how lonely each one remains in spite of being married to one another, or having fathers and mothers, brothers or sisters, and how at times I am able to ease this condition simply by sitting on their laps, coming when they call, lying at the foot of the bed or just being about, it gives me a most pleasant feeling in my stomach and starts me purring. And you need not be ashamed if this happens to you, too.

[124]

"But what is this human love like?" I hear you ask. "How are we to know when it is beginning to happen to us, so that we too can enjoy it?"

All I can tell you is that it is something they feel, and when they hold you in their arms or you are lying in their laps and they begin to stroke you gently, it flows from them into you and then *you* feel it. If it isn't there, you won't; I mean to say, if they are just stroking you or scratching you absent-mindedly, or because they want to entertain you and play up to you, you won't feel anything.

But every so often, in their need to give love as well as receive it, they will sometimes, like children, half squeeze you to death. Something will come into their eyes; the touch of their hands will change; and then willy-nilly you will begin to purr and your claws will work in and out as they did when you were kittens at our teats, and therefore happy. Sometimes the love in you for them will be so strong that you will seize them with your front paws, back-kick with your hind legs and bite them with your teeth, because that is the way *we* often express our feelings, particularly when they are connected with s-x. I have often thought that this human

"Some say it's salt on the skin. I say it's love."

love is also connected with s-x, except that in some way they seem to be able to manage to separate it, which of course, is why it is so difficult to understand. At any rate, if possible you should try to control the biting and scratching, remembering that, even though loving, they are also stupid and won't understand your behavior and will think you are returning evil for good. I am convinced that from this stems our reputation for being false and treacherous. Horus knows we have a few faults, but treachery and falseness are no part of them.

And be careful of this human love, for it can be more painful than being beaten with a stick. People often stop loving and leave one. We never do.

"... onto their stomachs."

"... by climbing up ..."

"You can often ease their loneliness ..."

CHAPTER XV

Two-Timing

I WANT MY READERS to know that I have undergone a good deal of soul-searching before embarking upon this subject. Two-Timing, or how to live in two homes simultaneously, is not very nice. It isn't something I am proud of, yet it does happen occasionally, sometimes through no fault of our own and, therefore, I feel that, even though I don't approve of it, it is something you ought to know, and in particular know how to go about should the situation arise.

Not long ago I happened to be speaking in a somewhat admonitory tone to a "smoke" who lives in our neighborhood and who has succeeded in convincing two separate sets of people that she is their exclusive cat. I must say in all honesty that her reply put rather a new light upon the matter. She said, "But think of the pleasure I am able to give to two families instead of only one. I am therefore twice as valuable."

Hence, I have decided to include a few remarks about the art and technique of Two-Timing.

My own recollection is that this custom actually began in wars, and had a practical foundation based upon the fact that very often there was not enough to eat in one house and so one went to cadge the second meal at another. However, people being what they are and demanding *quid pro quo*, they would become possessive in return for feeding one, and soon would begin talking about "Our cat who wandered in," etc. Thus the problem had to be dealt with.

"Shh . . . don't let anyone see you."

Two-Timing requires a profound knowledge of human nature and considerable study and experience. To be one hundred per cent successful, each family must be wholly convinced that you are their exclusive cat. And do you know when you may feel assured that you have achieved your object? It is when you will have acquired two names, one for each household.

Two-Timing, of course, is chiefly a matter of gluttony and feeding. If you don't get sufficient to eat in one house, or haven't been able to train your people to feed you the kind of food you like, but other things are satisfactory, you acquire a second home and thus can have two sets of meals daily. This can also mean two sets of toys, sleeping accommodations and interesting and exciting things to do, as well as various types of humans.

If you are bent upon Two-Timing you must, of course, choose a relaxed family from the very beginning, one that is sympathetic to, and understanding of, you as a cat and that won't fuss at absences from home, provided they are not too prolonged. I should say that forty-eight hours is the limit that you could remain away without arousing suspicion. Actually a twenty-four hour schedule is much better—one day and night off, one on—and can be maintained without too much exertion.

Naturally, then, your second family must be somewhat similar, though here very often you can pick up with a bachelor or a lonely widow, who will be so grateful for the fact that you have come to stay with them that they will not complain if you disappear regularly, always provided that you return and are careful to make yourself more than usually agreeable during those visits. People who travel or are away a great deal are excellent prospects for the double life. Of course the ideal combination, and it happened once to a friend of mine, is to find one home where the man is a night worker and hence sleeps during the day, and another keeping normal hours. This cat was able to work on a twelve-hour basis. But how often can one be so fortunate?

The smart Two-Timer very soon learns a few simple tricks connected with the habits of members of the two families. For instance, say one of them comes home from work at a certain hour every evening—you make it your business to be at the gate to greet him. He is so pleased and flattered at this that he pays no attention to what goes on afterwards, and there is nothing to keep you from nipping back immediately to your other family if you are in residence with them at that particular time. There are other equally simple subterfuges. If, for instance, the female of the house likes to have you around in the morning, be there. Nothing need stop you from spending the afternoon at the other place.

The beginning, of course, is important when it is necessary to be seen as much as possible in both houses. This means that for a time you may be kept busy charging back and forth between the two until they are convinced that you are there a great deal more than you are, while at the same time you are accustoming them to regular absences at certain hours. Human beings are absolute creatures of habit, and once you form those habits correctly you need have no further worries.

"And, of course, get a second handout."

You won't even, in some cases, have to become the exclusive cat of both parties. I knew a cat which lived with a modest, middle-income family. She used to call regularly at the mansion of some immensely wealthy people for handouts. The meals were provided by the butler, a rather lonely man whose free time was from three in the afternoon until six o'clock in the evening. My friend would accompany him to his room during these hours and sit with him, which was all he required. In return for this she got the most gorgeous treats, since the family for whom the butler worked ate only the most expensive things. The rest of the time she spent with her own family, of whom she was quite fond and with whom she was most comfortable. This family soon came to regard the hours from three to six as "Kitty's outing time," and nobody ever asked where she went or what she did. Here you have the ideal example of Two-Timing in its most beneficial form.

But you will have seen by now that not only are tact and intelligence called for, but chance plays a good deal of a part: the kind of neighborhood in which you happen to live, the district adjoining, and the class and condition of the people living there. You might go for a year or more quite content with one family and then suddenly become aware of an opportunity for a little Two-Timing that would hurt nobody, and with, as my smoky friend pointed out, a chance to make two quite different kinds of people happy.

I have kept to the very last one grave word of warning, to be strictly observed. Never, under any circumstances, permit your two families to meet, and above all, never let yourself be caught in the presence of both parties. If you have spent any time whatsoever with humans, you will know how extraordinarily sensitive they are about their possessions. Apparently one of the most powerful words in their language is "mine." Things they consider theirs, if they are in any way endangered, will stir them to depths of almost unbelievable ferocity.

I know of a story almost too horrible to retail, and yet I feel that for your sakes I must. It is of a Two-Timing cat that was so careless as to go to sleep in the sun by some public highway, apparently halfway between both her houses. By an unhappy coincidence the paths of members of her two families crossed at exactly that point. The cat, wakened by the violent altercation between them over her ownership, was momentarily too bewildered and befuddled by sleep to do what she ought to have done, which was to turn tail and flee as though the devil were after her. Before she knew what was happening, one family had her by the head and the other by the tail. *And pulled!* I think I need say no more upon the subject.

CHAPTER XVI

Errors

"All I can say is, don't do it."

"Shedding on the sofa is frowned upon."

WE ARE ASSUMING that, guided by this volume, you have been successful in taking over a household. The people therein, whether they be a married couple with or without children, bachelor or career girl, are absolutely soppy about you, consider you the greatest cat that ever lived and concern themselves with not only granting your every desire, but trying to anticipate them as well. In other words you are set for life.

Or are you? Yes, provided you do not grow careless and commit any one of a number of errors into which a house cat, particularly one who is being pampered and spoiled, can fall unless he or she is made aware of them by someone of experience like myself.

"This is fun, but does the screen door no good at all."

By using your head and, I hope, the precepts put forward in this textbook, you can gain entrance into any house. Never forget, however, that all doors are two-way and you can be chucked out even more quickly than you got in, and what is more, permanently.

And this may well happen to you, not because people are superior to you, but because they are inferior. They hate work, they dislike responsibility, they are nervous, lazy, irritable, and panic easily. Most of the time they don't know their own minds.

It is up to you to observe your family, smell out when they are nervous, and lay low during this period. For instance, when there is important company coming for dinner and the woman is fussing over the arrangements: the cooking, the setting of the table, the tidying up of the drawing room—this is the time to keep out from under her feet. Take a snooze, or better still go off somewhere outdoors where you won't even be seen, because at those times she may well take a dislike to you, not only for anything you could have done, like upsetting something or getting cat hairs on the sofa, but also for what you *might* do. This is a characteristic that is difficult for a cat to understand, but humans have the power to project their thoughts ahead. It is called imagination.

For instance, she has the table nicely laid. She sees you across the room, sitting with a reflective look upon your face, and instantly she imagines the havoc you could cause if you were to jump onto the table, or get your hooks into the tablecloth and pull—something, of course, you would never dream of doing. But that doesn't make any difference. To humans a deed imagined is often one already done, and it might well start the train of thought in her mind: "I really must speak to John tonight about getting rid of that cat. Goodness knows I have enough on my mind without having to worry about what some animal is going to be up to."

One evening you may find your man absolutely soppy over you, and the next, sharp and irritable, so much so that he may even give you a slap on your flank and shout, "Damn it, get down, Kitty! Can't you see I'm busy?"

Don't, I repeat *don't*, fall into the error of retaliation by insisting upon your rights at that moment. Something has gone wrong at the office or his wife has made a nasty remark or he has lost some money. Lay low. Get out of sight. Your rights are safe enough—even safer, because pretty soon his conscience will begin to work on him; he will feel guilty that he struck you and shortly after will apologize with some tempting tidbit, and afterwards he will be soppier than ever.

Need I mention cleanliness, and I don't mean just washing, but making messes? Only to say that a well-bred house cat will *explode* before she will soil a rug or the floor. If you feel you are going to be sick and are shut up in the house with nobody

"Not a very bright idea. Some people are fussy about their silly birds."

"A for Effort."

there to let you out, go and be sick in the bathroom. That's where they go, and you will have become familiar enough with the place to know where it is and what it is for. Even if you cannot help making a mess on the bathroom floor, they will give you "A" for effort, and because they do think of you more as one of themselves than an animal, they will say, "Oh, poor Kitty. She did try to get to the can." Any kind of a mess on the mat or in the drawing room will inevitably start people thinking along the lines of what life would be like without a pet, and this is the last thing ever that you will want them to do, because they will suddenly remember freedoms which they had before you took over, freedoms from worries, responsibilities, etc., and before you know it, you are on your way out.

CHAPTER XVII

Games and Recreations

Including Fireside Reading,

Letter Writing,

and Small Household Repairs

THE ABOVE CATEGORIES don't refer to yours but to theirs, and they are not to be tolerated unless you, yourself, have something better to do. Any indulgence by your people in the above must be on sufferance and with your permission. You must establish firmly and quickly, once and for all, that they are not to participate in any of

"THIS we are going to have to break up!"

"This is how it's done."

"You may want the dictionary, but I don't want you to have it."

them if you happen to want attention. Under "games" we consider any such pastimes as scrabble, dominoes, chess, checkers (and in the old days, mah-jongg), card games of any kind, ping-pong, badminton, etc.

Every well-educated house cat ought to know when and how to break them up. For instance, there is no point in interfering with a scrabble game at the very beginning. They will only shoo you away, and if you persist, throw you out or shut you up in another room. Such procedure shows not only lack of instruction but failure to appreciate the psychology of people, which, in a house cat, is a far more serious defect. The proper method is to wait until the board is practically full with a most complicated arrangement of words. *Then*, jump up onto the board with the most sweetly saccharine "Purrrrrrmaow" that you can muster, scatter the pieces in all directions, sit down, and commence to wash.

They will be absolutely furious with you for a moment, but never forget they are potty over you, or they would never let you get away with everything you do in the house. It will be too much trouble for them to try to remember the words they had formed, or the pattern of the letters. Hence it will be far easier to skip the whole thing and pay attention to you, or go and do something else.

The same goes for dominoes, chess, checkers, parchesi, snakes and ladders, and anything at all with a board and movable pieces. Scatter the pieces. Sit on the board.

Ping-pong, of couse, is a setup. The first time the ball hits the floor, fall on it, tackle it, pass it, dribble it, juggle and run with it. They will instantly become far more interested in watching *you* at play than in playing themselves. And, incidentally, this is an excellent and simple way to teach them how much you enjoy a ping-pong ball and to get them to supply you with your own, which you will keep amongst your toys.

Card games are more difficult to break up, with the exception of Solitaire, where you are dealing with only one person, who is bored and lonely or he wouldn't be playing Solitaire, which means that you are halfway home. When you see that he has a game nicely laid out, jump up onto the table and sit on the cards. If he attempts to push you away, push back, rubbing up against his hands, arms, or shoulders and purring violently. You will see, he will give up the game because, apparently, your need for companionship is greater than his.

Interfering with a bridge table or a poker session is much more difficult and, actually, not advisable, and no smart house cat will attempt it, though it can be done. It is much easier to prevent two people from having a quiet evening of relaxation and entertainment than to break up an organized card party with a house full of guests. To do so, to stop all activity and center it upon yourself, you must actually provide more entertainment and novelty than may be had from the cards. In other words, clown it to the extent where you lose dignity and the game is no longer worth the candle.

When you see your person settle down to do some fireside or after-dinner reading, jump up into his or her lap, get comfortable, and then put your paws across the book or paper. This will make turning the pages difficult, and after a while you will find they will give up.

"Don't mind ME, ha ha! Go right ahead and read."

"Make passes at the pencil with your paw . . ." *". . . or simply lie down on the writing paper."*

Letter-writing is even easier to break up, since none of them really and truly want to write letters. Here you use a more direct technique, which is to get on the table or desk and lie down on the writing paper. If they persist, begin to make little passes at the pen with your paw, as though it were a game. In the old days, before they all had mechanical pens, we used to upset the ink bottle, which was most effective, even though it sometimes got us into serious trouble, but the lesson of the overturned ink bottle was never forgotten. Still, today if you will continue to play with the pen, eventually the letter writer will say, "Oh, Kitty, you are a nuisance," but it will be said, actually, with relief, for it means he can put off writing letters still another day with a clear conscience.

I find I have forgotten to mention another interference, which can be the greatest sport. Many people don't use a pen or a pencil, but instead a machine known as a typewriter, for writing letters or even doing work. If you are so fortunate as to happen to have chosen an author to live with, you may spend the most delightful hours interfering with his effort, for which he will be most grateful to you, since every author I have ever heard of will seize upon the slightest excuse to avoid writing. And, at the same time, you can have a marvelous game yourself.

[141]

The principle of the typewriter, you will soon learn, is that as the author presses down a key on the keyboard, a bar bearing a letter rises up from its innards and strikes the paper. *Your* game is to see whether you can be quick enough with your paw to catch the letter before it strikes the paper. It is glorious sport and wonderful exercise, and one of the best things about it is that you can play even when the author is not there, for you can press down the key yourself with one paw and go for the bar with the other.

But to return to preventing the writer from getting on with his work. As soon as he sits down at the typewriter, climb into his lap and start the game. Never wait until he has begun or becomes interested in what he is doing, for then your task will be more difficult and you might even suffer the indignity of being thrown out into the garden or shut up in the kitchen. You will learn that it is exactly at the moment when he sits down at the typewriter that he is at his weakest and can be most easily put off, for it has taken a tremendous effort for him to bring himself to the point of getting down to the machine.

Interfering with small household repairs, wallpapering, or paint jobs is not only useful in keeping your family properly disciplined, it can also be great fun. You can sit on their tools, upset boxes of nails, insist upon playing with bits of string or wire that are being used, and, of course, if a wallpaper job is being undertaken, you first lie on top of the paper, then you can go under it and pretend you are a ghost, and if they still won't cease and desist and begin to pay attention to you, shred the paper, which is, of course, the greatest fun of all.

The easiest household activity to put a stop to is when the woman of the house gets out her sewing basket. At some time or other your family will have played the string game with you, dangling a bit of twine before you or pulling it across the carpet, and into which you will have entered, not for their amusement, but because it is good exercise and excellent for keeping your eye and your timing in. Well then, they can't complain if, when they produce needle and thread and begin making the same motions as in the string game, you join in. Watch out for the needles, they are sharp; go for the thread. There is also a great deal of mileage to be had out of upsetting the sewing basket, which will result in a satisfying cascade of balls of yarn, spools, thimbles, scissors, etc. Don't, I repeat, DON'T be put off by being given an empty one to play with. Insist upon having the spool of silk or cotton *they* want to use.

Similar techniques apply to persons who indulge in needlework, tatting, tapestry-making, or knitting. Knitters are particularly vulnerable with their balls of wool. If you are clever about it, you can get the ball unrolled clear across the room or even

"That ends work for that day."

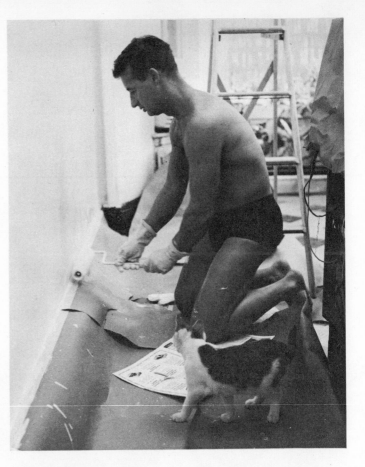

"After a while you will find they give up."

down the stairs and onto the next floor before they know what is happening. This usually will suffice to finish the knitting for the day.

There are many other activities of people, not covered here, that you will encounter, and if you have mastered the basic techniques as I have outlined them, you will be able to improvise to suit every occasion. I have a friend, for instance, who found to her surprise one evening that she had taken over the home of a stamp collector, when he brought out his book of stamps, loose specimens, sticky papers, bowl of water, etc. A cleverer-than-most pupil of mine, it did not take her long to see that here was the most fortuitous combination of things she had learned. She sat on the album, scattered the loose stamps, upset the water, and rolled in the sticky papers. I can tell you, this soon put a stop to *that* business. Another recent pupil of mine earned my commendation by her behavior the first time she encountered her mistress doing a jigsaw puzzle. She not only was clever enough to wait until the puzzle was four-fifths complete before upsetting it, but also had the good sense to carry off several of the pieces and hide them.

Whatever you do, once you have started to interfere with one of their activities, never stop until they have given up for the day. In this way you will form proper habits for them, and eventually they will learn to ask your permission before attempting anything.

[144]

"Cinch! I'll have this unravelled in a jiffy."

"Eventually they will give up playing their games and come around

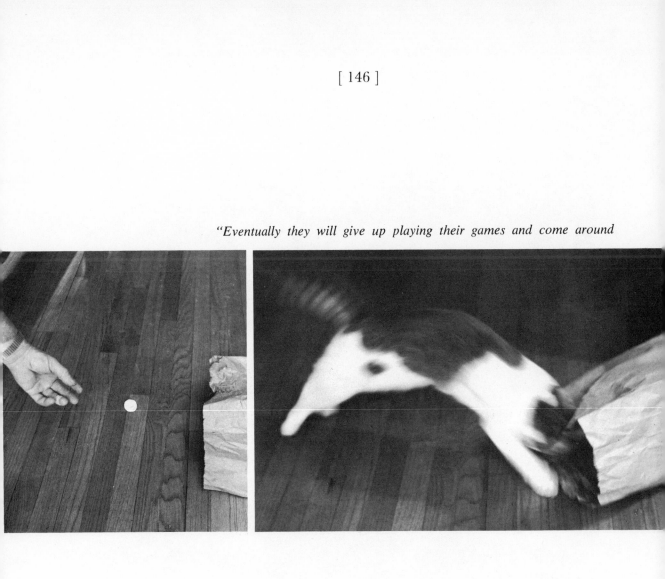

to playing yours. *This one happens to be one of my favorites."*

CHAPTER XVIII

Preparation and Training of the Young

ALTHOUGH THIS BOOK has been written for kittens, strays, the homeless and the young, this particular chapter is addressed to rather more mature cats who have already found homes, who are perhaps in the family way or might possibly become involved in such a mishap. You will have noted, I am sure, that in my chapter on motherhood I gave no advice whatsoever upon the raising and training of kittens.

"I certainly didn't teach this one to interfere with my food."

"The proper way to eat." "The proper way to play." "Already used to beds."

"They have learned their lesson on attitudes."

"All ready for the take-over."

"Look at this one cuddle."

"Three to go."

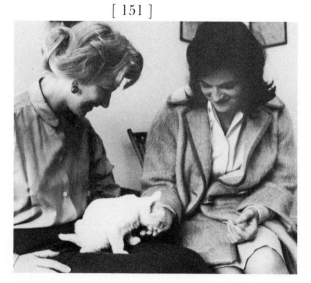

*"How's this for a con artist? This one's got
it made."*

What cat is there who needs such advice, who does not know instinctively how to
look after her offspring properly and efficiently? And, believe me, we do a better
job than humans with their own young, as surely you must have remarked if you
have had anything to do with some of the beastly, ill-mannered, and bad-tempered
ones they have managed to produce. Leave our kittens with us from four to eight
weeks and we will turn out worthwhile cats every time.

"That leaves two."

"See my lesson on traveling."

But if you have read through this book carefully, you will have gleaned that in this day and age being an ordinary barn, field, or house cat is not enough, and that it no longer suffices to raise kittens properly toilet-trained, with good manners and the ability to look after themselves. Today, with living space shrunk to small apartments, bungalows, prefabricated houses, etc., the servant problem completely out of hand and the competition for homes and a life of ease for us cats fiercer than ever, our kittens must be taught from their infancy how to con the members of the human race.

For the same situation that I have just outlined is making it more and more difficult for a cat to find house room, and likewise impossible for you to be allowed

"This one will have no problems."

"I've taught her not to fuss when held like this . . ."

". . . and to pick comfortable spots to sleep."

to keep your kittens. If you think you are going to be any exception, you are just a fool, and I have no further time to waste upon you. No, your family will be planning to get rid of them as quickly as they possibly can. It is up to you, then, to see that they are taught from the very beginning all of the ways and means of bamboozling their two-footed friends and taking them over, in addition to the usual virtues we inculcate into our young.

If you are an expectant mother you will do well to review my chapters on attitudes, speech, manners and errors, and the first thing you should teach your kitten, or kittens, is how to look piteous and helpless, a gambit that works particularly well for them. A cat my age trying this one would merely seem ridiculous, but a kitten

"Last one—and doing its job."

[153]

"This one's a bit young, but never mind, my kitten will soon teach her."

taught to appear properly miserable and frightened can often win a home at first inspection.

They should be taught the Silent Miaow before the vocal one, as well as all of the expressions on their faces that people like to think are human, but in particular you should prepare your kittens for the immediate take-over of children, since it will be these who will first be called in to scrutinize them. I have already touched upon children in my chapter on people. Even as your kittens will know instinctively that they must pounce on anything small that moves, they must today realize almost equally instinctively that little boys and girls are acquisitive, selfish, aggressive, thoughtless, demanding, greedy and obstinate. They have also a constant need for attention, and any animal that will flatter them by giving them a lick or cuddle, rub-up or a purr, is two-thirds home. The other third of the way is accomplished if the child can be made to give vent to its battle-cry of "I wanna!"

For the parents of these little monsters are for the most part indulgent, blind, pampering, complacent, yielding, coddling, accommodating, inclined to spoil, weak, lenient, easy-going and long-suffering. *Your* human family knows all this very well or they wouldn't be inviting other people's children around to see the kittens, and if they are smart enough to know this, so should you be.

Never mind whether at first your kittens understand everything you are teaching them. If you begin at a proper age, which I consider to be when they open their eyes, they probably won't. For the time being it is sufficient to let them merely memorize the list of human frailties which will be so useful to them in later life, and which you and I had to learn the hard way, by experience; their self-adulation, vanity, fears, insecurity, unreliability, ego, etc. The list is, of course, far too long to be absorbed in one or two lessons, but in a matter of a few weeks any kitten can be taught the names of these traits and how to recognize and make use of them.

[154]

Believe me, *my* four kittens were ready and thoroughly instructed almost from the time they could walk, and I'm proud to say that we didn't lose a single child of the four that came to see them when they were considered old enough to acquire homes of their own.

My first one took over a little girl by going limp on her and behaving exactly like a rag doll, one of the primary things I had taught her. Number two, the white one who looked like his father, did the perfect snow job on an older girl by giving her hand a lick or two, a ploy which you will also find in this book and will have made use of yourself. The third got another little girl first time out, simply by attitudes. This one happened to look like me, and so had no difficulty in appearing sweet, charming, and irresistible. The last one wasn't even a fair game. The child was so young he took the kitten for another like himself and we were in. Four at-bats, four hits, four runs.

In a way, of course, I was sorry to lose them, but then in another, I wasn't. I was so very proud of them and of myself for the education I had given them.

Besides which, from then on I was again boss in my own home, and no more kittens, thank you.

"Look who's boss again. ME!"

CHAPTER XIX

Conclusion

VOMVLUS8ON

9 jope tjst $ou 2ho habe resd rhis b99k wikk jave haimed dometjing grom ut. Ib comxlud8on 9 qoulf day ti eve4y kotteb tjat

EDITOR'S NOTE

The above from the last page of the manuscript translates as follows:

CONCLUSION

I hope that you who have read this book will have gained something from it. In conclusion I would say to every kitten that

Unfortunately the world will never learn what the author wished to say to every kitten in conclusion, for in some manner the final chapter had been damaged and the rest missing, except for the opening lines quoted above. I cannot think what further admonitions could be added to the foregoing, and if there was a final summing up of the human species as seen through a cat's eyes, it is probably just as well left out.

Having completed the translation of the manuscript, and realizing the extraordinary nature of the find, I confess that I hesitated a long time before returning it to the publisher, and indeed, at one time I contemplated destroying it.

For a good deal of this cannot help but come as a sadly disillusioning revelation to hundreds of thousands, perhaps millions, of cat owners who believe that they are just that—cat owners. Particularly in the Anglo-Saxon countries, the United States and Great Britain, Kitty is an established member of the family and is so accepted. What are regarded as her little foibles, or "ways," are tolerated with good humor and understanding, and to use one of the author's pet words, anthropomorphism.

But the general belief is that it is we who have taken in Puss and permitted her to share in our lives. It must come as something of a shock to learn that the whole thing is a vast, intricately woven and thought-out plot, and that when we look with comfort and pleasure at our Tabby curled up in her favorite chair, or sitting in a corner looking contemplative, we must now be prepared to admit that we have been really euchred out of the use of that chair and the sweet reflection upon the face of our pet masks what next she is planning to sucker us into or out of.

On the other hand, I thought, perhaps the disillusionment would not be all that severe.

The conclusion toward which I am leaning is that in all probability the majority of cat people, deep down, have a sneaking and half-recognized suspicion that they have been taken over by their feline, four-footed friend and that to a considerable extent she has imposed her whims and wishes upon the household. One hopes, then, that to have it thus confirmed will do no more than stir that sense of humor without which no one can really enjoy the company of cats and simply substantiate the gentle tyranny to which they have already voluntarily submitted.

My publisher friend upon whose doorstep the manuscript was originally deposited, seized upon it avidly when I had told him the gist of its contents and was even more eager to produce it once he had read it through. For, himself an ailurophobe, a cat-hater, he was certain that this *exposé* would open the eyes of the philes, or lovers, and enable them to see cats in their true light.

"This will fix those panhandling little so-and-sos," he chortled, and ordered the manuscript rushed to the printers, in spite of my warning him that it would not have the desired effect; on the contrary, ailurophiles one and all would only love them the more for their cleverness. And, after all, this book is only one cat's opinion.

Besides, what is there in the final analysis so disillusioning or shocking about it? In a way it seems to me a useful handbook for cat owners as well as "kottebs," and points out the short and easy road to a happy and peaceful life with one's pet, which, after all, is the end aim of any relationship between two humans as well as human and animal.

It is resistance to the inevitable that causes friction. A man goes contrary to the wishes of his woman and the sparks fly, until he is cozened, trained or mechanized to be more amenable. Had some such handbook as this been available to him in his youth, he would have recognized immediately that he was bound to be out-smarted by the female of his choice and accepted his status from the very beginning with the tolerance and self-mockery that one expects of the genuine dyed-in-the-wool cat person.

And then there is that curious and surprising chapter and commentary upon human love, as described and interpreted by an animal who has either chosen or been conditioned to live with man instead of its own kind. There is a cry of pure anguish at its conclusion: ". . . be careful of this human love, for it can be more painful than being beaten with a stick."

If this will arise to smite the consciences of those who, having lived with cats, will suddenly abandon them, or leave them behind because of expediency or sheer laziness, this unknown author will not have written in vain.

Besides which, the human failing to resist truth and accept only what it wishes to believe will, I am sure, survive even these revelations. The other morning, after my cat, Sambo, a smoky gray, had been missing for two days and two nights, I encountered him walking up the road from the direction of a neighborhood where the houses are far larger and wealthier than mine. With my work in translating *The Silent Miaow* fresh in my mind, I was moved to suspicion immediately. Was Sambo two-timing me? In what mansion on the right side of the railroad tracks was he being fed, pampered, and accepted as belonging to them? A momentary pang of fierce jealousy shot through me, to be instantly dispelled. Sambo two-time me? Not *my* cat!

I picked him up, chucked him under the chin, and asked him where he'd been. He put his foot in my mouth, rubbed his head against my face, and began to purr violently. There was no point in pursuing the subject further. He was obviously, as always, absolutely mad about me.

PAUL W. GALLICO

Photographer's note

WHEN CICA FIRST APPEARED at the window of our summer barn in Westhampton, L.I., a mere handful of seductive kitten, little did we suspect her iron will to adopt us. Two peripatetic photographers just *can't* have a cat!—we said.

Besides being so charming and tenacious at home, Cica's take-over extended even to the car, for which she had the most unusual fondness, and, of course, she had to be in every picture we took. Luckily she turned out to be such a wonderful photographic subject. Nothing is more important and refreshing for a professional photographer than a new and compelling subject: a continuous inspiration to the kind of work that is also pleasure.

And so Cica became entrenched. What started out as pity for a poor, homeless kitten, and as a photographic challenge, became a rewarding relationship. Nevertheless, despite Cica's propensity for modeling, this book would not have been possible without the collaboration of my husband, Ray Shorr, who took all the pictures in which I appear with Cica. Ray, himself, for the first time in his life—and unquestionably, now that we understand it, under the influence of Cica's guile—discovered what it was like to become the subject of a picture story. I think he is still besotted.

We both trust that Cica is now going to be the most famous cat in the world. One disturbing thought, though: Will Success Spoil Cica?